THE PARENTING MANUAL

Simplified Instructions For Raising
Happy and Thriving Kids

by Doon Baqi

Typesetting by Kelley Creative. www.kelleycreative.design

ISBN 978-1-7331088-0-5

Contents

Foreword

This long-awaited manual serves as a guide to the current capabilities and future potential of the Human Child, Model 249 (referred to herein interchangeably as "child," "children," or simply the "HC"). We will present research-based scientific results and best practices to be applied by the Human Child Parent(s) ("parent," "parents," or simply the "HCP") for an easy to use instruction manual. We state now, and shall reiterate multiple times throughout the manual, that the HCP should seek out the actual studies and research for themselves in order to gain a deeper understanding of the subject matter and to stay abreast on any updates to the science.

Today's HC is highly versatile and plays an integral role in the propagation of our species, and can thrive in a variety of environments, from the remote mountains of Afghanistan to the sandy beaches of Australia, and all the way to Virginia, on the eastern seaboard of the United States of America.

This manual highlights training principles, child capabilities, and parenting methods, techniques, and standards that apply to the modern HC. It also strives to provide preliminary instructions during the HC's incubation period, and offers a number of graphics, tables, and other relevant charts to facilitate training. If this information conflicts with any other applicable technical manual (TM) currently in circulation, the HCP team is urged to undertake its own further research operations using Google, the library, or any other information acquisition sources in order to find the most recent, relevant, and peer reviewed research on the matter. HCP teams should feel at liberty to modify the manual's instructions to meet their local conditions and/or individual child and family's needs and nuances.

In all cases, HCP teams must evaluate their standing approaches to parenting in order to ensure adherence to the building-block principles of child rearing presented in this field manual. It is not necessary for an HCP team to be perfect in the application of every aspect of this manual in order to be successful, perfection is hardly attainable in any pursuit, and raising a HC is arguably one of the most difficult endeavors of the human experience. This is a learning process, and there will be many mistakes along the way. The key is to strive to improve, and the intention is for this manual to assist in paving the way.

Parents will find herein a range of issues to explore. Some parents, for example, may want help in determining what to consider in setting up the child's physical space for best intellectual development. Some may want to know when math instruction should begin. Are there things parents can do to boost a child's memory and mental development? What are the best approaches to child discipline, and what sort of limits and boundaries should be placed on the child? These issues and many others will be presented in this manual. In order to simplify the manual and not bog it down by a ton of data, the authors have intentionally left out the details of the studies that relate to the concepts. Again, HCP teams are encouraged to thoroughly research the concepts that they learn here. In the process of parenting, advice is aplenty and comes from all directions. Parents should also research that as well and ensure the advice is research based and meets the rigorous tests that the scientific community applies.

It is incontrovertible that parenting is incredibly challenging, but it is just as incontrovertible that it is incredibly rewarding. We wish all parents the best of luck.

Notes:

Unless this manual states otherwise, feminine nouns and pronouns do not refer exclusively to women, and male nouns and pronouns do not refer exclusively to men.

For the purposes of this manual, and unless specified otherwise, an "HCP team" refers to one (or more) handler(s)s (aka "parents" or "guardians") in any sex and gender configuration (i.e. M-F, F-F, M-M, etc.), and at least one HC.

CHAPTER 1:
INTRODUCTION

THE HUMAN CHILD IN HISTORICAL PERSPECTIVE

Human children have been an integral component of human species propagation since ancient times. From the very beginning of the human experience, the rearing skills and methods applied by parents have served as an important component of the survivability and the final personality disposition of the HC. Indeed, parenting techniques and styles have often served as predictors of the type of adult the HC will become.

Over the millennia, the HC has proven itself to be a highly sophisticated and versatile extension of the parental unit itself, serving not only as a means of facilitating the survival of the parental genetic code, but also being a resource both financially and emotionally for the aging parents, often extending the lifespan of the parents by many years beyond the age of natural expiration. Children are an important component of the human experience, and as of the drafting of this field manual, there is nothing that can replace the HC's effectiveness in species survival and overall joy for the human experience.

THE HUMAN CHILD PARENTING TEAMS

The HCP team is an essential factor in proper HC development. The methods of parenting may have evolved over the millennia, but the role of the HCP team has remained constant: to assist in early life survival, provide sustenance, and shift to training and societal preparation as the HC matures.

The HCP team's individual composition can come in a variety of configurations. While single parenting is certainly sufficient, and most HCP teams have historically consisted of a two-parent team, often one male and one female, there are no hard and fast rules for this. Regardless of the sex of the parents, they will often find that there is plenty of help around. Friends and relatives often pitch in, thereby breathing life to the axiom that it "takes a village" to raise a child.

Since parents play such a crucial role, in order for the child to thrive, parents should also strive to be healthy. A physical, emotional and spiritual well-balanced HCP team will be in the best position to handle the vagaries of raising children. Therefore, this manual will also offer techniques and suggestions to help the HCP team be its best in meeting the challenges of parenting.

CHAPTER 2:
THE ARRIVAL OF THE
HUMAN CHILD

This section of the manual contains information useful to the HCP team during the child's incubation period as the team prepares and plans for the arrival of a new baby. It is not only first-time expectant parents that will benefit, but also those already working with at least one child.

Weeks or even days prior to the baby's arrival, parents will find themselves deep in the "nesting" phase as they finalize preparations. There is much anticipation, excitement, and fear ahead. The training and preparation process specific to the individual HCP team will vary based on many factors, and the suggestions in this manual should be treated as general guidelines rather than absolute mandates. As always, HCP teams are encouraged to conduct their own research to ensure these tips are applicable to their individual family's needs.

PREPARATION AND THE INCUBATION PHASE

The initial shock of learning of the pregnancy will soon give way to a range of emotions as diametrically different as rapture and fear. Like a well-played Ping-Pong match, parents may feel this emotional back-and-forth until the moment of birth, and quite frankly it is likely to continue into the parents' deathbed. It is no wonder that parental gray hairs experience a rate of proliferation exponentially greater than their non-parent counterparts.

Read on, haggard parents. This manual will also help you stave off the effects of this early onslaught of.

THE DISCOVERY

Parents will discover that they are serving as an incubation unit for another human being in a variety of manners. We will not concern ourselves with the causes of the incubation, as this manual endeavors to focus on the maintenance of the incubation once the process has already begun. But suffice it to say that the resulting incubation, whether intentional or, as is frequently the case, the result of happenstance, will change everything.

At some point, the HCP team will become aware that changes are afoot. One of the earliest signals is the cessation of the menstrual cycle. As many women keep meticulous records of the cycle, irregularities can often be detected immediately.

Many women may also experience a number of physiological effects associated with pregnancy. These could include bloating, gas, sore breasts, cramping, fatigue, nausea, constipation, mood swings, fatigue, or a metallic taste in mouth. It is important to note that the number and intensity of these symptoms vary from one woman to another, and there is no set of predictors that would consistently confirm the pregnancy. The gas and bloating, for example, can simply be a result of the previous night's low-grade tequila and the concomitant consumption of greasy hangover food. Or it can be caused by some other illness or poor diet, stress, or numerous factors and should be discussed with a physician.

Once the HCP team suspects that there may be a child in the cards for them, the next step may be an over-the-counter pregnancy test or a visit to the primary doctor for confirmation.

THE ANNOUNCE

While the initial reaction may include shock and panic, accompanied by an instinctual rush to find the nearest dark cave in which to hide, the expectant parents will eventually come to terms with their new reality and move on to more practical tasks such as debating the time and method of sharing the information with the world. Many couples decide to delay the announcement until the end of the first trimester because of the increased risk of miscarriage during this period.

Below are factors to consider when deciding whether to share the news, even if not yet past the first trimester:

- **First trimester help:** because the symptoms are especially severe in that first trimester, the pregnant mother can receive help from friends and family as she copes with morning sickness, fatigue, and whatever other feelings and emotions she may be experiencing.

- **Support network:** parents can begin early in the creation of a support group, receiving help with the baby registry, planning the baby shower, and so on.

- **No secrets:** many families avoid keeping secrets, and would prefer to share the news with loved ones so that things are out in the open.

- **The unspeakable:** if the unspeakable were to happen, the support of the community can be of great help to the grieving parents.

NESTING

Much as the rest of the animal kingdom prepares for the arrival of its spawn, so too parents will engage in various nesting activities in the weeks prior to delivery. We will discuss a few of the general guidelines and suggestions, but as with most every other topic in the manual, an entire separate publication can be dedicated to this phase, and parents are urged to conduct their own research and find something suitable that fits their own lives. Below are a few things to consider:

The Crib

Unless the parenting unit has managed to command a budget sufficient for expert installation, the task of assembly of the crib will be theirs and theirs alone, with the male traditionally doing the actual assembly and the female assisting/supervising (although this configuration by no means is or should be the standard for the division of labor). In addition to the work involved in assembling, factors to consider in buying the crib include:

- Cost of crib

- Size of crib and availability of space

- Whether it has an adjustable mattress height. Upon baby's first arrival, a higher setting allows for ease in placing the sleeping child into the crib, but as the baby grows, parents may want the option to lower the mattress to avoid the child falling and/or crawling out.

The Car Seat

Arguably one of the most important items of inventory, the car seat installation process can be a nerve-racking experience. Does one install it facing forward, backward, does one place it on the side near the window, in the center, in the trunk? These questions have perplexed parents for centuries and no doubt will continue to do so until some inventive parent creates self-installing car seats. Until then, parents should consult the American Automobile Association (AAA) or a nearby police or fire station for guidance. Below are a few factors to keep in mind when considering buying a new seat:

- The vehicle's owner manual for location and how to install

- The correct type for the age of the child (rear facing for the first two years, forward facing and booster seats as the child grows)

- Ease of cleaning. Parents will soon discover that the crevices of the car seat will attract items never before seen by the human eye

- The existence of cup holders

The Pump

The breast pump will be a major source of sanity for the mother, especially in those first few exhausting months of the baby's arrival. Not only will it give the father a chance to bond with and participate in the feeding of the baby, but it will also allow the mother a much-needed opportunity to rest from the three-hour sleep cycle the baby will demand in order to feed. Indeed, a banked supply of milk can also give the new parents an opportunity to leave the baby with a family member and step out of the house for a few hours of essential bonding time.

The Baby Monitor

If budget permits, the baby monitor, especially if equipped with a camera, can be quite useful. No longer bound to constantly monitoring with the naked eye, parents can enjoy a semblance of normalcy while the baby sleeps as they catch up on those missed Netflix shows. A good baby monitor is a very practical investment and high on the list of recommended purchases.

SEX OF THE BABY

There is widespread debate on whether to find out the sex of the baby prior to actual delivery. This is an entirely subjective matter for the expectant parents, and a number of factors should be considered when determining whether to do so:

- **Painting of nursery**: the parental unit may want to know early in order to know what color to paint the room. And while the dichotomy of pink and blue has taken our selection colors by siege, there is no reason that compels parents to adhere to this fairly recent assignment of colors. Indeed, it wasn't too long ago when pink was the masculine color and blue the feminine. This distinction is arbitrary. And these colors are not the only choices available, but much to the chagrin of the rest of the color spectrum, manufacturers of toys, clothing, and furniture have honed in on these two colors only. Parents should also consider the other colors on the spectrum and not let this be a deciding factor in whether to learn the sex.

- **Baby names**: while there is some crossover in names, especially European names (e.g. Pat, Chris, or Ray), most names are gender specific, and as such, parents may need to come to an early consensus on the name in order to avoid the stress of finalizing in the last minute. A suggested strategy is for each parent to propose a list of ten names to the other, and then select three names from the partner's list, making it six names in sum (three from each). These six names are then written on small pieces of paper, which in turn are crumbled up and tossed into a bowl whereby a sibling if one exists, will draw a name as the first name, and another as the middle name. There are plenty of other approaches to name selection that a cursory Internet search can reveal. Nonetheless, parents should do what suits them.

"BABY MOON"

Parents are advised to take one last small trip prior the arrival of the baby, perhaps a weekend getaway if possible. Ensure that the destination is cleared with the physician, and that it is not very far from the hospital should the child decide, as it is often wont to do, to arrive early. Discuss with a doctor any travel restrictions and recommendations and adhere to them. This may be the last opportunity for alone time in quite a while.

IN SUM

The incubation period is an important time for parents as they prepare to meet the new member of the team. Revel in this preparation phase. Be present and document the steps and emotions. The child will eventually want to know what life was like prior to her or his arrival.

A checklist for the new baby:

- ☐ Baby monitor

- ☐ Diaper Bag

- ☐ Diapers

- ☐ Diaper chaining pads

- ☐ Dirty diaper receptacle

- ☐ Wet wipes

- ☐ Cream

- ☐ Crib

- ☐ Bassinet

- ☐ Car seat

- ☐ Blanket

- ☐ Clothes

- ☐ Pump

- ☐ Swaddle

- ☐ Small bath

- ☐ Nursing pillow

- ☐ A comfortable nursing chair

- ☐ Baby nail clippers

- ☐ Baby shampoo

- ☐ Cotton swabs

- ☐ Digital thermometer

- ☐ Bulb nasal aspirator

- ☐ Mild soap for laundry

- ☐ Stroller

- ☐ Baby books

- ☐ Baby toys

- ☐ Good luck!

CHAPTER 3:
THE FOURTH TRIMESTER

As the date approaches, parents will undoubtedly find themselves brimming with impatience. And when the baby finally does arrive, the new parents, especially and inevitably the first-timers, may be a bit overzealous. They will approach things with an overabundance of caution, standing sentry in the delivery room doorway, hovering close by to ensure every visitor applies globs of antibacterial soap before even glancing at the child. This will undoubtedly annoy some of the older visitors, especially as they may have clear memories of "back in their day" or "back in the old country" where such antics were unheard of and "babies could be delivered in stables and still turn out fine." It will not help to point out that those relatives making such claims have likely never been near a stable, much less delivered a baby in one. Parents may also face a bit of mocking on that initial journey home from the hospital, often in the far right lane, as they are drive at a glacial pace at or below the posted speed limit signs for the first time since learning to drive with their driver's ed teacher in high school.

Parents should be prepared to endure such ridicule especially from the Human Child Grandparent Group (HCGG), because such ridicule will likely continue for as long as you have HCGG units.

COLIC

Once the baby has arrived at its new living quarters, it will have to undergo a major adjustment period in the new physical environment, having spent its entire existence thus far in a tightly encapsulated, warm, and wet space, in the gentle sway of the mother's amniotic fluid, and the loud whooshing sounds of her blood flow. There will be much to adjust to, least of which is the din and the flurry of activity of people constantly hovering over it. The new world will consist of strange new creatures who are nothing more than blurry outlines against an alien background that is cold rather than the warmth from which it comes, bright rather than dark, and kinetic rather than the calm of the womb. In addition, the baby must now expend energy in order to get energy, where it once merely existed and was fed with no effort. There will be a lot of frustration as it tries to find the right angle to latch on to its mother's nipple, sometimes a difficult process for both mother and child as they seek a position that is effective for child and not painful for mother.

It is no wonder then that the baby will be overwhelmed with all sorts of new challenges and anxieties, leading to fussiness and irritation and what is sometimes diagnosed as "colic." A baby has been said to have colic if it fits the rule of threes: the baby will cry for three or more hours a day, for at least three days a week, and for three consecutive weeks. Parents should consult with their pediatrician to ensure there is nothing medical that causing discomfort. However, more than likely, the diagnosis will be colic. There is no consensus as to what causes colic, and theories have been put forth ranging from digestive issues (lactose intolerance, for example) to the child's innate ability to sense the parents' anxiety. There has been no definitive proof one way or another, although there is some research that points to a greater risk of colic with mothers who smoked cigarettes during pregnancy or postpartum.

With that said, parents should take comfort as colic will usually peak at around 6 weeks, and gradually go away by the time the child is between three and four months of age. As much as the cause of colic is a mystery, one particular pediatrician named Dr. Harvey Karp has emerged as a bit of a "baby whisperer" with regards to the inconsolable baby and has an interesting theory as to the root cause of colic. Dr. Karp surmises that the human species, being at the top of the food chain, is distinguished from all other creatures, at least on earth, as having an especially large cranium to body ratio. As such, the birth of the human child must occur earlier than the babies of other species in order to allow for the oversized brain to exit the mother's body without causing significant damage or even death to her body.

Most animal newborns are capable of walking almost from the moment of birth, but the human child needs a much longer period of care before it is self-sufficient. Dr. Karp has theorized that, but for the big head, the human child would otherwise have remained in the mother's womb an additional three to four months (roughly the timespan of a trimester), and thus that human children generally arrive an entire "trimester" early, which Dr. Karp has dubbed the "fourth trimester." It is for this early arrival that the baby displays high levels of anxiety and discomfort associated with colic. The baby longs again for the womb where it experienced constant warmth, gentle swaying, the soothing whooshing of the mother's blood flow, and the familiar tight confines where it wasn't bothered by overbearing aunts and uncles who simply refuse to let it sleep.

In other words, the baby wants to go back home. And as a card-carrying member of the human species, it has an innate need to communicate with those around it. Since its vocal muscles have not yet developed sufficiently (at least with regards to speech), it has at its disposal one very effective means of communicating this newfound discomfort (as well as other basic needs): crying. It can be quite jarring for new parents to hear their child wail in the middle of the night and not be able to mollify it. But parents should take some comfort in knowing that this is normal behavior. While the rest of the human species uses millions of words to communicate their anxieties and desires, the infant has but one word - the cry. An infant's cry can be quite meaningful, and parents will eventually pick up on its nuances. In no time, parents will be able to discern between the various sounds, and learn that the baby is trying to communicate to the parents one of the following:

• Its diaper needs a change

• It's hungry

• It needs to release gas (burp or eructation)

• It's not feeling well (and needs a doctor)

• It's frustrated

• It's tired (this crying is often late afternoon or early evening to release tension after a long day)

Colicky babies are certainly a source of extreme frustration and worry for parents, but there may be some help.

THE FIVE S's

Once the newborn is exhibiting the signs of colic, first thing parents should do is to immediately attend to those basic needs (diaper, food, burp, and so on). More often than not, this will be sufficient to calm the child. But if the baby continues to cry despite having been examined for pain, changed, fed, and burped, then the parents should turn to what Dr. Karp calls the "Five S's." As discussed above, the newborn has just left a womb where it spent its first nine months of life in a tight, dark, and warm space, gently swaying in amniotic fluid and surrounded by the constant soothing sound of its mother's gushing bodily fluids. The "Five S's" attempts to recreate that environment in five consecutive steps and usually results in a placated baby. Parents are encouraged to read Dr. Karp's book, *The Happiest Baby On The Block* for a detailed explanation of when and how to apply the technique. Below, is a brief summary of the steps, which should be followed in order:

1. **Swaddling**. The first "S" is swaddling, the snug wrapping of baby using a thin blanket or cloth. Dr. Karp's recommended

method is to wrap both arms along the body in order to avoid the flailing arms from hitting and startling the baby, thereby restarting the crying. Swaddling is the first step in recreating the beloved womb environment, and will not only begin the soothing process, but also prime the baby for the next four S's. The proper technique is illustrated below, but parents are urged to obtain a copy of the book and accompanying instructional DVDs to better understand the method:

2. **Side/Stomach Position**. While on its back is the safest and preferred position to put a baby to sleep, Dr. Karp says that it is the worst for soothing it when it is in its crying hysterics. After the baby has been swaddled, parents should thus hold the baby on its side or stomach. This is the second "S" and will make the baby more receptive to the remaining S's.

3. **Shushing**. The next "S" is "shushing." As previously discussed,
    the first nine months of the baby's existence is not one of
    silence. Rather, it is filled with the constant steady sound of
    the internal orchestra of its mother's body, the ultimate white
    noise sound machine. From the beginning, the baby hears
    the constant shushing rush of blood throughout the mother's
    body, amplified in resonance by the excellent conductivity of
    the bones and the amniotic fluid. These internal sounds may
    also combine with the muffled blurry sounds of the outside
    world, creating a constant whooshing sound that lull the
    baby into sleep. Then, as it so happens, the baby is suddenly
    and without warning evicted from the womb and thrust
    into the bone-chilling silence of the outside world, and it is
    harrowing. The poor baby hears echoes, it hears the breeze,
    it hears an ambulance, and it hears the haunting yet piercing
    sound of its own voice wailing into the silent night. This is
    the very opposite of the gentle lulling hush of its motherland.
    It is no wonder then that recreating the sounds of the womb
    miraculously quiets the angry beast. Some parents turn on a
    vacuum cleaner or drive a car around the neighborhood, but
    it is often sufficient to place one's mouth next to the baby's
    ear and simply "shush" loudly into the ear until the child is

calmed. Contrary to what one might think, it is not a gentle quiet sound, but loud and somewhat forceful and helps drown out the rest of the world's cacophony. For those with smartphones, there are a number of apps that have a variety of sounds (such as rainfall) that come close to mimicking the womb sound. A swaddled baby, held on its side or stomach, being shushed in the ear will usually calm down, but if not, move on to the next step.

4. **<u>Swaying</u>**. Just as life inside the womb is not quiet, it is also not very still. It is fluid and kinetic. The baby is constantly moving like a piece of Jell-O, and Jell-O is the very image Dr. Karp suggests you keep in your mind as you gently sway the baby who is swaddled, being held on her side or stomach, and while she listens to the shushing in her ear. It is very important to note that this swaying is absolutely not shaking, and parents should look up instructional videos on how to perform this step. Shaking is positively doing it wrong and can be very dangerous to the baby. The motion is a gentle Jell-O-like sway.

5. **<u>Sucking</u>**. The final "S" is "sucking." As evidenced by the proliferation of pacifiers, an infant's calming reflex is triggered when it has something in its mouth to suck on. Clearly, an evolutionary adaptive behavior intended to help it survive (i.e. feed), having a pacifier nearby is the final "S" and will likely be all that you need to be known as a baby whisperer yourself. Once the baby is swaddled, held on her side, shushed, and swayed, gently insert a pacifier in baby's mouth and chances are that pre-baby silence will return to the home.

IN SUM

The proper application of the 5 S's will usually result in a quiet and calm baby. If not, it is often the result of incorrect application of the 5 S's and parents should review the methods in order to refresh their memories and then reapply them. If the problem persists, parents are again encouraged to contact a doctor to ensure that there is no serious medical condition such as milk allergy, ear infections, or some other potentially serious malady. It should also be noted that sometimes nothing will soothe the beast, and we have but one thing to say to you: welcome to parenting.

CHAPTER 4:
SLEEP

Humans need sleep for survival. With age, the need for sleep decreases. In this chapter, we will discuss the importance of sleep, and strategies in coping with a baby who wakes every few hours, as well as methods of sleep training employed by thousands of parents to teach the baby to sleep through the night. The loss of sleep is the one thing most parents of newborns complain about, but with a little patience, this too can be conquered.

SLEEP BENEFITS

Infants have an overwhelming need to sleep. This is a blessing and serves as an excellent opportunity for parents to catch up on their own lives. But in addition to parental recovery time, sleep also serves a number of important developmental purposes for the child, extending well beyond infancy and into toddlerhood and beyond. It is during sleep that the body initiates its self-regulating maintenance checks, evaluating the previous day's experiences and mending itself. Most of the child's growth regulation takes place during sleep, especially in the deepest stages of sleep, during which the human growth hormone is abundantly released. In addition, hunger regulation takes place during sleep, and the body releases various hormones to monitor and regulate appetite and blood sugar levels. Studies have shown that sleep deprivation leads to greater hunger and thus greater caloric consumption.

The child's brain is also hard at work during sleep, reorganizing and consolidating memories and the day's received information.

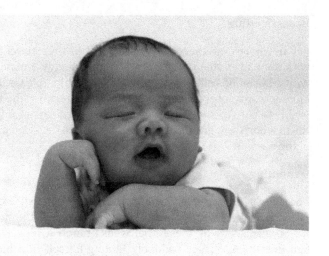

Scientists are learning that the benefits of sleep actually extend beyond the physical and emotional. Recent research has discovered a strong correlation between sleep and success in academics. Indeed, studies of children raised in impoverished households show that these kids tend to do worse in school primarily because of the quality of sleep they get. The cacophony of the sound of sirens and airplanes and cars not only disrupts sleep, but also may even elicit a stress response whose pernicious consequences are well documented. With so much happening during sleep, it is paramount that parents ensure children receive adequate amounts of sleep.

NEWBORN SLEEP

The newly arrived baby will normally have little to no consistency in sleep patterns, and its sleep cycles are driven almost entirely by hunger. While the rest of the household may be on a normal human sleep cycle, the infant could not care less and will wake at any hour it wants to ask, that is to say, cry, for food. Parents can expect this at minimum every two to three hours. Establishing a sleep pattern therefore for the newborn will be difficult during the first three or four months.

Breastfeeding

For newborns, mothers are encouraged to breastfeed to help with the baby's sleep. The normal human body regulates sleep with a hormone called melatonin, increasing its release into the bloodstream closer to sleep time. By breastfeeding, the mother is able to pass this regulation mechanism through her milk onto the newborn as it gradually begins to replicate the sleep patterns of the mother.

Swaddling

The newly arrived baby will have spent the final weeks of pregnancy confined in a very tight space inside the mother's womb, especially as these final weeks found it bigger than it had ever been. Then, suddenly finding herself in a big, cold, and unfamiliar world can be jarring. Newborns will have not yet developed the motor skills needed to control their flailing arms and will often experience what is known as "startle events," uncontrolled jerks of the body, which are especially pronounced during sleep. These startle events can wake the baby and affect the quality of her sleep. Parents are thus encouraged to swaddle when putting the newborn to sleep to prevent the flailing of the arms. It is important to note that a baby should be placed only on its back for sleep, as any other position can be highly dangerous and lead to suffocation.

Sleep Training Exercise

While the newborn's hunger is the primary driver of its sleep patterns in the initial weeks and months, at some point (usually at around six months), it may behoove parents to initiate a sleep-training curriculum. While the parents' natural tendency is to rush to a crying baby and remain with her until she is calm, parents are encouraged to teach the baby the self-soothing process whereby it soothes itself to sleep, both in the initial falling asleep phase as well as in the middle of the night when s/he abruptly wakes. This "self-soothing" skill will not only provide a sanity break for parents, but will also benefit the child later in life, providing the ability to fall asleep in just about any environment. While there are many different sleep training programs, the Ferber Method, described below, has consistently been shown to be effective.

The Ferber Method

Dr. Richard Ferber created a very effective method to help babies learn to self-soothe. It involves a gradual reduction of soothing by parents, which ultimately results in a reduced reliance on parents for sleep. While simple in words, the technique may require a Herculean level of self-control by parents as they struggle to restrain their powerful instinctive urge to rush to the crying baby's side. This will require both parents as it may become necessary for one to physically restrain the other from getting up as the baby's wails pluck at every string of the heart. To reiterate, the Ferber Method is not for newborns, and a child should have reached around six months of age before initiating the process.

The general steps are as follows, but parents are encouraged to conduct their own research and adapt it to their individual families:

1. After routine time, put the baby down for sleep. Soothe it, say goodnight, and then walk away and leave the room if possible.

2. The baby may feel distressed at this point. Let her fuss and cry for about one minute.

3. Return to the baby and soothe her.

4. Once she has calmed, leave the room again, this time for a longer period of time, perhaps three minutes.

5. Gradually build up to leaving the room for 30 minutes or more. It is in this phase that one or the other (or both) parents will need to be restrained so as not to rush to the baby before the designated time is up.

6. After two or three days of crying for 30 or 40 minutes, the baby will eventually and hopefully stop crying and fall asleep on her own.

7. Parents will then be free to bask in the feeling of elation. A bottle of wine is highly recommended at this point to celebrate the milestone.

ROUTINE AND RITUALS

Once parents survive the newborn phase, they should consider a nightly routine and ritual. Research has consistently demonstrated the effectiveness of a bedtime ritual for children, and providing regular and predictable physical and sensory cues to that effect can help establish proper sleeping patterns. Parents are encouraged to feed the baby at the same time whenever possible. There should be a nightly ritual established, consisting of feeding, bathing, playing gentle familiar music, dressing in comfortable pajamas, and reading one or more books as the child gradually winds down. Parents should avoid offering any television or screen time stimulation during this time, as the images and light emitted from the screens can trigger a wake response in the human body, thereby disrupting the human circadian patterns, which in turn will push the window of sleep back by as much as an hour. While there is plenty of room for deviation from the proposed routine to fit individual needs, below is a suggested list:

1. **Bath**: An hour and a half prior to bedtime.

2. **Book**: An hour prior to bedtime, begin reading.

3. **Brush teeth:** Half an hour prior to bedtime, brush teeth (if teeth have arrived).

4. **Song and cuddle**: Ten minutes prior to bedtime, snuggle, wind down in bed, discuss the day's accomplishments, and perhaps end with a lullaby.

SUGGESTED SLEEP REQUIREMENTS

The following table is a general sleep requirement guideline for children, but a pediatrician should be consulted for the individual needs of the child:

- **First month**: 16 hours (including naps)

- **Until end of first year**: 14 hours

- **Through end of the third year**: 12 hours

- **Through the age of 12**: 10 hours

Parents are encouraged to closely scrutinize any charts that suggest different amounts of sleep, as some describe the number of hours of sleep children actually get rather than how much they should be getting.

ADDITIONAL SUGGESTIONS

Human children thrive with adequate amounts of sleep, proper routines, and sleep training. If a child is a bit too irritable or tired, then parents should monitor the child's sleep patterns to find places for adjustment, perhaps, for example, by shifting bedtime up by half an hour and observing the results. They should also ensure that children get at least an hour of exercise or play every day, which can help drain energy and make falling asleep easier. It is also recommended that, to the extent possible, the child avoids staying up past bedtime even during the various social activities (such as weddings or other family gatherings) that are often scheduled past bedtime. This helps maintain proper sleep patterns.

IN SUM

In summary, parents are encouraged to:

- Swaddle a newborn prior to bed.

- Breastfeed a newborn to pass the mother's melatonin-producing mechanism to the baby.

- Establish early a routine with consistent familiar physical and sensory cues and stick to it as much as possible.

- Follow a sleep-training method like the Ferber method to teach the child to self soothe.

- Avoid screens prior to bed.

- To the extent possible, try to adhere to the sleep requirement guidelines.

CHAPTER 5:
DEVELOPMENT - INFANCY

From early infancy through adulthood, there are a number of steps that parents may take to enhance the child's developmental progress. While some methods may be limited by budgetary restrictions, there is ample opportunity for al parents to provide a developmentally rich environment in which the child can thrive.

TUMMY TIME

Until very recently, children were placed primarily on their stomachs to sleep. Recent research, however, has linked this position to suffocation since the baby's mouth and nose can become blocked by loose bedding, and the baby's neck muscles are not yet strong enough to lift the head out of the way. Most pediatricians now recommend only putting the infant to sleep on her back, especially in the initial months. This shift to sleeping on the stomach has resulted in a small delay of the start of crawling, although most children's locomotion does tend to normalize by the eighteenth month. To accommodate for this delay, parents are urged to give the baby regular "tummy time" in those early months.

There are a number of developmental benefits associated with tummy time, which then leads to crawling and independent locomotion, providing the infant ample opportunity to explore its world. At around two months, parents should place the infant on her tummy for a few minutes each day. The two or three-month-old baby may initially resist this and fuss and cry. The baby is still in the early stages of neck and back muscle development, and this may initially prove a bit uncomfortable for the baby. Parents are encouraged to pick up and soothe the baby. After a few minutes, try again, gradually increasing the time it spends on its belly each day. Eventually, its awkward and uncoordinated jagged movements will transform into coordinated crawling as the baby begins to explore the world around it. And simply put, the more it explores, the better for its cognitive development.

As the baby develops and grows, the crawling will evolve into the "cruising" stage during which it grasps couches and other objects in order to keep itself upright, which will ultimately lead to its first independent steps. During each of these stages, parents should take extensive care to remove any dangerous objects from the baby's cruising path. A number of retailers provide soft cushioning material with an adhesive to attach to the sharp edges of furniture to prevent injury. Wall sockets should also be

covered up, and of course, poisonous items such as household
cleaners should either be locked up or put out of the child's reach.

SITTING UP

Parents are encouraged to purchase a sitting aid like the Bumbo
product (www.bumbo.com).   At about four months of age,
parents may choose to place the baby in it for interaction. While
there is a lack of scientific research supporting any cognitive
benefits from this soft cushiony chair, the baby may benefit from
sitting up, freeing hands to interact with various objects and
people surrounding them.

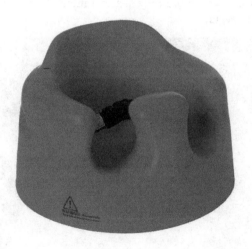

STIMULATION

Even though an infant may not yet be ready to take advanced math
and physics exams, a number of studies have found that young
infants have a basic grasp of addition and subtraction, gravity,
and inertia. For example, in one study, infants watched a ball roll
across a table and bump into another ball, thereby causing the
second ball to roll. Then, the experiment was repeated and they
watched the first ball roll and come to a stop just shy of touching

the second ball, and yet the second ball was manipulated by the researchers and made to roll away anyway. The infants would look significantly longer at the second ball, aware that something was amiss. Similar experiments were performed with gravity and simple addition and subtraction.

Stimulating Environment

Therefore, it is important to provide children with a richly-stimulating social and physical environment in which they can interact with various people and objects of all shapes, sizes, colors, and textures. What may be visible on the outside is a tip of an iceberg of the information processing taking place in the baby's brain. The more they see and interact, the better their brain will develop.

Studies have shown that an infant has more synapses in its brain than an adult, and thus a more dense plexus of brain cells. By providing the child with ample opportunity to play with a variety of objects, these synapses are activated and the infant develops faster. But while variety is encouraged, simplicity should be the guiding post. Although some parents may rush out to buy gimmicky stimulating toys with sirens and flashing lights, there is no research to support that these have greater benefits than a more simplified object such as a wooden block. A book with simple pictures, for example, is superior to a book with sound effects and lights.

Physical Interaction

Along with tummy time, infants can greatly benefit from physically interacting with their environment. Parents are encouraged to play simple games with the baby to help along in the process. An example of simple play is gently rolling a ball towards the infant several times so that it can learn to anticipate the ball's position and perhaps reach out and try to catch it. Place toys just out of reach so that the baby can reach for it and try to grasp it. These seemingly trivial activities light up the neuronal plexus.

Sticky Mittens

In the early days of life, the infant's motor skills are far from developed, and tasks as simple as holding on to an object are nearly impossible. Parents can make sticky mittens by attaching Velcro tape to a sock or mitten and the other half of the tape to a soft toy so that the baby can grasp the toy, which is sure to bring lots of fun and stimulation to both parent and child.

Baby Walker

At some point, the infant will crave to become mobile. Parents should research the safety of individual brands and models, but in general, a walker is a good investment. By providing a pre-locomotive infant a level of mobility, it can lead to dramatic mental and cognitive development.

IN SUM

The first few months of a child's life are incredibly important in terms of cognitive development. Parents are encouraged to:

- Practice regular tummy time at around the third month.

- Practice sitting up at around the fourth month.

- Provide ample stimulation, including games, sticky mittens, and a baby walker.

CHAPTER 6:
DEVELOPMENT - BEYOND INFANCY

As the child matures and gains more control over the environment, the level and type of stimulation must evolve along with it. As the child gains mastery over its motor skills and becomes more mobile, parents are encouraged to introduce new challenges to maintain the development progression. In this chapter, numerous activities are presented as suggestions. The limitations of time and money will certainly dictate which and how many of these the parents can incorporate into their lives, but the more of these the better for the child.

MARTIAL ARTS

A large body of research continues to link certain physical activities with greater cognitive benefits, and martial arts is one of the biggest contributors. As the child grows older, parents are encouraged to enroll the child in some sort of disciplined physical activity, such as any one of the martial arts. The majority of studies involve Tae Kwon Do, a Korean martial art that has gained a lot of popularity in America, but the benefits should extend to other forms of martial art as well. In the experiments, school children were separated into two groups over a period of a semester, one group's physical activity was composed entirely of Tae Kwon Do, and the other did physical training traditionally taught in schools. The group that was enrolled in Tae Kwon Do tested better in standardized math tests and also behaved better in their classrooms. They showed an improved level of the ability to remain focused, resist distraction, and regulate their own emotions, and ultimately increased certain "prosocial" behaviors such as sharing and better cooperation.

PATIENCE

Likely for similar reasons as martial arts, improving the child's ability to exercise patience has been shown to have great cognitive benefits. Perhaps made famous by the Marshmallow Study in which children were given the choice of one marshmallow now or two later if they were able to wait for ten minutes. There was a link with future success tied to the children who were able to wait the ten minutes. Parents can exercise the child's patience muscle at home. When the child asks for something, certainly give the item, but parents should periodically delay the actual handover, perhaps telling the child that the parent is preoccupied for a minute and that the child should wait. Gradually, the span of time can be increased to two or even three minutes before finally handing over the requested item.

MUSIC

There is ample evidence that learning music can increase the size of the brain. Studies have linked learning music early in life to better results in a variety of tests, including IQ tests and those that test spatial skills. Roughly at around the age of five, parents are encouraged to enroll their children in some sort of musical learning classes in which they actually learn to read music. There is no one instrument that benefits more than others, but the trick is to ensure that the lessons involve learning to read notes, which can in a way serve as a whole new language for the brain of the child.

IN SUM

As the child continues to grow and the brain matures, parents are encouraged to continue to provide ample stimulation to maximize cognitive development. Activities such as martial arts, patience building, and music lessons are some examples that are research supported to help in this regard, but parents are encouraged to find other things that are better suited to fit their temporal and financial restrictions. The important thing is that the child continues to receive mental stimulation.

CHAPTER 7:
STORYTELLING

STORY TIME

A basic tenet of the human child-training program is story time. The telling of stories has been a survival mechanism for our species from the onset of human speech. In those early days, it was stories that served as the conduit for valuable battle lessons learned on the African savannah. Storytelling has stayed with us throughout the history of our species. It is therefore no wonder then that the child can benefit from appropriate and effective stories. Not only does storytelling engage the parent with the child, but it also stimulates the child's imagination, leading to various cognitive benefits.

Story telling can come in handy for parents in many situations. Provided that the parent has sufficient bandwidth in the day, the story can be used, for example, on long drives in lieu of screens, or in the restroom as the parent waits for the child to expunge daily waste (gas mask recommended). In addition, story telling can come in handy while waiting in line at the grocery store and certainly in the lulling minutes before sleep. It is an invaluable tool that should be used as frequently as the parent has patience. The creative process may seem daunting, but as most Hollywood writers have learned, there is actually a simple basic template that most stories follow. Below is a simplified version of this template.

The Protagonist

It is important to keep the child engaged in the story, so it behooves parents to present the child with a few initial choices. The first decision to be made by the child is whether the protagonist is a human, an animal, or an animated inanimate object (such as a talking car). Stories are also an excellent opportunity to present to the child a glimpse into the parent's own childhood, and the protagonist of the story can be a younger version of the parent telling the story to describe some aspect of the parent's childhood or past.

Parents should name the protagonist, and it can be helpful to invent a name that is a close rhyme of the child, with a few letters modified to create psychological distance (Katherine can become "Flatherine," and Zohra can become "Flora," for example).

The Plot

Once the protagonist is established, the next step is to decide the type of story to tell. While there are numerous plotlines to choose from, below is a basic list of stories that generally resonate with children:

- **The Quest**. This is a classic plot in which a hero goes out into the world and searches for something. To be effective, the hero's ordinary world leaves the hero incomplete and lacking something, which the quest will remedy. The hero sets out into the world in search of this thing, encountering various setbacks along the way, each bringing the hero closer to the goal. In the end, there is a major discovery or clue that leads the hero to the final goal.

- **Revenge**. In this story, the hero's ordinary world is a strong place of comfort and wellbeing. Then, there is a disturbance to this world and either the hero or someone the hero cares about is wronged. The hero then goes on a journey to first identify the wrongdoer and then seeks out to find the culprit. These stories end with the hero finding the wrongdoer and bringing him or her to justice.

- **Adventure**. The hero in this tale sets out on a journey, but unlike the quest story, the object of the journey is not anything in particular other than the adventure itself. The hero's ordinary world may seem dull and boring. Along the journey, the hero encounters many strange people and creatures and somehow grows from the experience.

- **The Chase**. Due to some real or perceived danger, the hero is on the run in these stories. Often it is because of a terrible mistake and the hero has to run to get out of a bad situation. At some point, the chase comes to an end and the hero sets the record straight, thereby able to return to the ordinary world.

Most of these tales, whether oral stories, written, or audio/visual (television and film) follow a rather simple skeletal structure. Once this structure is mastered, it can serve as a template for nearly any type of story, and parents simply plug in the various tent poles of the particular story to captivate the child. Below is a general yet simplified structure outline taken from Joseph Campbell who was an influence in structuring the Star Wars movies among countless others:

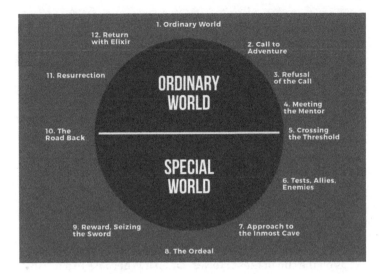

1. **Ordinary World**: Here, the hero is introduced along with
    the world in which the hero resides. This is a world quite the
    opposite of what the hero will encounter in the adventure
    ahead. There is often something lacking in the hero's life.
    Think of Luke Skywalker's life with his aunt and uncle on the
    desert planet before the arrival of the droids.

2. **Call to Adventure**. Then some herald arrives and brings
    some new information that is meant to draw the hero out of
    the ordinary world. In Star Wars, this was the droids.

3. **Refusal of the Call**. For a variety of reasons, there is always
    an element of reluctance for the hero to mobilize on this
    adventure. This reluctance must always be expressed by the
    hero or someone else.

4. **Meeting with the Mentor**. After refusing the call, the hero
    meets with some mentor figure that may give the hero some
    sort of talisman or tool to help in the journey ahead.

5. **Crossing of First Threshold**. Finally, the hero agrees to
    whatever was asked of him or her by the call to adventure.

Or, alternatively, the hero is pushed into action and has no choice. Luke is attacked on the planet and must act.

6. **Belly of the Whale**. The hero suddenly finds herself in a whole new world. In this stage, the hero must quickly learn the rules of the new place and may undergo some initial training. The hero encounters a series of tests to see if she can survive.

7. **Tests, Allies, Enemies**. Along the way, the hero meets various new people, some who will become friends and allies, and others who will be the opposition. Luke's journey leads him to Yoda, Han Solo, and so on.

8. **Setback**. At some point, the hero encounters some major setback, where the hero is left to question the entire purpose of the journey and may come close to giving up, but doesn't. Luke's near loss in the garbage box.

9. **Ordeal**. The hero finally has the major battle or ordeal and often using whatever was given to him or her by the mentor is used here to defeat the villain. Luke's battle with Darth.

10. **Back to Ordinary World**. Once the mission has been accomplished, the hero returns to the ordinary world a changed person, reflecting on all that has transpired, and bringing back whatever they have gone out in search of.

Life Lessons

Parents can use these stories to pass on all sorts of information. From simple anecdotes to major life lessons, stories can be used as a very effective tool to supplement other teaching methods. As a suggestion, parents may benefit from reflecting on the day and finding an area in which the child may need some additional guidance, and then creating a story to serve as the conduit of the lesson. For example, if the child had trouble sharing on that day, the story can be about a frog that learns to share in order to make its world a better place. The possibilities are limited only by the imagination of the parents.

Whether dealing with a toddler or an older child, the story can be modified to best suit the situation at hand. Younger children may require a one-off story in which the beginning and end will be encountered in a single telling. Older children may require something a bit more complex, and the parents will have to make the story into a serialized tale, telling the story in its entirety spread out over many nights.

Multiple Children

There are times in which parents may have to tell a story to more than one child whose ages may be years apart. In this situation, it is best to introduce a character for each member of the audience, alter the names as previously discussed, and have multiple parallel stories contained in one story.

CHAPTER 8
SCREENS

The amount of time that children spend in front of a screen has been shown to be directly correlated with the child's intellectual, physical, and emotional development. Research has consistently proven that the risks of screens are many and the benefits few.

FLASH CUTS

Most television programs move fast and have rapid cuts from one scene to another, hardly permitting the viewer to have sufficient time to focus on any one image. Studies have shown that this fast-paced flashy programming can reduce a child's ability to focus on simple problem-solving tasks. In addition, it can reduce a child's ability to avoid distractions. Parents should avoid these kinds of programming altogether, but especially near bedtime or near the time that the child has to work on challenging homework assignments.

VIOLENCE

There is ample evidence to show that a child's exposure to violent television shows is linked to aggressive and violent behavior with peers. Researchers have also linked violent programming with children's violent and aggressive reactions when faced with various ordinary real-world scenarios. From a scientific perspective, the human biological response to seeing violence is the triggering of the fight or flight mechanism. When the exposure to violence is regular and repeated, humans habituate and become desensitized to the violence. What should be regarded as abnormal becomes seen as ordinary. Indeed, research showed that children who were repeatedly exposed to violent programming showed a greater frequency of negative thoughts and a drastic reduction in sharing. Parents are thereby encouraged to screen beforehand what shows children watch, and to limit violent programming.

INFANTS

The American Academy of Pediatrics (AAP) has issued multiple recommendations on the matter of infants and screens, specifically stating that, "Television and other entertainment media should be avoided for infants under age two." Parents are advised to strictly adhere to these guidelines. While it can be awfully tempting to use the screen as a pacifier or babysitter in order to get something accomplished, parents should remember the strong correlation between screens and poor cognitive development. Indeed, there is no evidence suggesting any positive effect of screens for children under two. In this regard, it is important to remember that previous generations were able to make do without it, and the wellbeing of the child is important enough to keep her away from screens.

BACKGROUND TELEVISION

Leaving the television set on in the background has also been found to have negative effects on children. Indeed, there is a body of evidence that suggests parents tend to engage much less with their children when background television is turned on. The more children under two years of age are exposed to adult programming (i.e. television playing in the background), the lower they score on cognitive tests by the time they have reached the age of four. For the sake of the child, parents should keep the television off while the child is in the room.

VIDEO GAMES

There is no blanket prohibition on video games, and indeed parents are encouraged to permit their children to play two to three hours of video games a week. They have been shown to have a number of positive correlations not only with the child's perceptual and cognitive development but also with self-esteem. Some research has linked the playing of video games with an increase in creativity. There is also a positive correlation with visual-spatial reasoning, which tends to lead people to professions in chemistry, mathematics, and other sciences. Video game play has also increased a child's ability to better pay attention to his or her current surroundings.

With that said, however, sustained video game play has been shown to have a negative correlation with the child's ability to hold attention on a task, a skill quite different than the awareness of surroundings, attention, and skill. In addition, parents are encouraged to limit the type of video games, as there is a similarly strong negative correlation with playing violent video games and aggression and violence. Indeed, not only do such children become more violent in school, they tend to perform significantly worse in school and get lower grades.

SCREENS AND OLDER CHILDREN

While a reduction in screen time is certainly recommended, a complete prohibition may not be feasible, especially as children grow older. Therefore, parents are advised to limit the daily exposure to screens to less than two hours, ideally striving for only one hour. One parent's method to keep tabs on how much screens are viewed is for parents to distribute every morning four small tickets or 3x5 cards, each representing a 15-minute block of time. Label them "screen cards," and if there are multiple children in the household, color-code them, a separate color for each child. At the start of the day, the child has four 15-minute blocks to view screens (one hour in sum). The child can use it in any fashion he or she wants to watch any pre-approved show or play any pre-approved game. At the start of each 15-minute session, one ticket is handed in, thereby buying the next 15-minute session of screen time. This method not only helps parents track the amount of screen time, but can also develop a child's time management skills. There are also various apps that can monitor the amount of time children play on phones and tablets.

LOCATION LIMITATIONS

To help manage screen time, parents can also use location limitations.

- **Bathrooms**. An effective rule to help limit screen time and simultaneously encourage reading is to prohibit the use of screens when the child is using the latrines (especially with older children who will spend a half hour at a time on the toilet to watch a show).

- **Drives**. On drives, screens should be banned for any journey that takes less than two hours. If the journey is to last beyond two hours, then at the two-hour mark, the child is handed a screen for an hour, and then back to no screens for another hour.

- Parents should place a basket of books and activity magazines within arms reach of the toilet and the car seat to enable the child to engage mentally. Both of these are excellent situations for parents to practice their storytelling skills. (A gas mask is highly recommended during the latrine story time sessions.)

RECOMMENDED PROGRAMMING

Parents are advised to avoid showing children programs that are fast-paced and flashy or shows that contain violence and/or adult programming. Instead, parents should opt for slower paced educational programming which can help the child to learn to read, get an early start on math, and become a better problem solver. While the screen inevitably takes away the child from social interactions, parents should make time to watch the programming with their child and discuss what they see. Below is a short list of some suggested programming:

<u>Under 5</u>

- Pingu
- Sesame Street
- Between the Lions
- Daniel Tiger
- CyberChase
- Little Einsteins

<u>Under 8</u>

- Wild Kratts
- Odd Squad
- Dino Dan
- Dino Dana

IN SUM

Parents should limit exposure of the child to screens. The AAP recommends that parents create "screen-free" zones where the child will have no exposure to television (active or background), video games, and other types of screens vying for attention. Over time, screen consumption will increase, but parents should not give up on their role of influencing the developing habits in the years that there is still influence.

CHAPTER 9:
PARENTING STYLES

EFFECTIVE PARENTING STYLE

There are generally three primary leadership styles, and the particular leader's style can be identified fairly quickly. The demands of life may require quick decisions that can impact lives. Scientists have divided parenting into leadership styles as well. For parents, the styles are divided into the following four categories: **laissez-faire** (uninvolved), **empathetic** (permissive), **cooperative** (authoritative), and **authoritarian** (just plain mean). While a brief analysis of each style is in order, it is recommended that all parents adopt the authoritative (cooperative) approach for best results in enhancing the child's cognitive and social development, as well as overall wellbeing and happiness.

Each parenting style can be measured by the degree of control the parent has over the child's behavior as well as the amount of warmth towards the child. A number of scientists have also studied the effects that each parenting style has on children, with the unequivocal conclusion that the **authoritative** approach produces the best outcome.

To demonstrate the various styles, consider the following situation as we go through each style: A seven-year-old child comes home from school, kicks off her shoes, and rushes to the restroom. Later, the parent sees the shoes out of place, and the parent's response will vary depending on the parenting style.

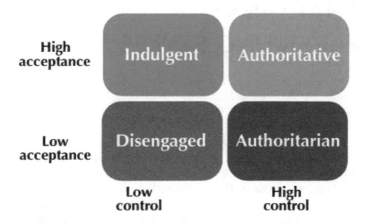

AUTHORITARIAN

On one end of the parenting spectrum is the drill sergeant approach in which the parents insists that his or her way is the right way, and no alternative of thought exists. The only permitted child response is, "Sir, yes sir, may I have another?" Any request for an explanation by the child for having to perform a particular task is usually met with a 'Because I said so' response which extinguishes any opportunity for discussion. This approach's primary process of shaping child behavior is through intimidation and punishment (or the constant threat of punishment).

The general perception of the authoritarian parents is that they are cold and not always in tune with a child's particular emotional needs. They score very high on the control meter, but particularly low on the warmth meter. The child raised in this environment is generally well behaved and gets into less trouble at school, and indeed tends to do better academically.

These kids, however, also tend to experience a greater amount of anxiety and depression as children as well as into adulthood. Socially, they may experience greater anxiety and generally feel like outsiders around their peers.

In the scenario of the child and the shoes, the authoritarian parent immediately imposes a punishment. "But dad," the child protests, hoping to explain that she urgently needed to use the restroom right then and that she intended to get back to the shoes, but simply forgot. The authoritarian parent peremptorily silences her and imposes a harsh punishment for breaking the rules.

LAISSEZ-FAIRE

On the other end of the spectrum is the uninvolved parent who, as a whole, doesn't seem to be interested in the child's development. This could very well be as a result of some internal issue with the parents, such as depression, or that they may merely be parenting the only way they know how, which is to duplicate the style of their own parents. This approach essentially deprives the child of the parental guidance children so very badly need in order to navigate the obstacle course of daily life. The uninvolved parenting style scores lowest both on control and warmth, as it is difficult for an absent sun to radiate warmth.

In the example of the girl and the shoes, the laissez-faire parent simply isn't paying any attention to see the out of place shoes. Not only is the child not reminded of the rule, but also no consequence is faced.

PERMISSIVE

Parents who have adopted the permissive approach to parenting tend to impose little or no limits on behavior, are often only presenting explanations for why the child should behave a certain way, and rarely insist that a child behave a certain way. From the permissive parent's perspective, children will thrive best when they learn to impose their own limits on behavior. While scoring very high on warmth, parents that adopt this approach will score low on control. The child raised in this environment tends to have more behavioral issues, typically having much more trouble at school. Based on the research, these children tend to watch a lot more screen time, are much more likely to be obese, and will have a higher likelihood of problems with alcohol and drugs as they get older.

In our example of the seven year old girl and her shoes, the permissive parent sees the shoes, and the girl explains about the exigency of the bathroom At this point, both go on with their own business, and no more is said about the matter, and the shoes are still not put away.

AUTHORITATIVE

A balanced middle ground for parenting style approaches is the cooperative approach, otherwise known as authoritative parenting. Parents are encouraged to adopt this approach, bringing an effective harmony between parental control and warmth. Parents should set clear limits and be the bulwark of those boundaries, especially since children tend to regularly test those boundaries. When children do push against the boundaries, parents should maintain a high level of warmth and respect with the child, and provide simple and clear explanations for the limits imposed. Indeed, involving the child in the creation and imposition of the limits allows the child to internalize and better understand the limits. Parents remain understanding of the idiosyncrasies of the situation, but also consistent in their enforcement of the rules. And while the child may not entirely understand the explanation provided, especially in the earlier years, research seems to indicate that it is the very act of taking the time to explain things that provides the benefits. Like children raised with each of the other parenting styles, children raised in a authoritative household may still experience problems at school, social issues, or problems in adulthood (such as depression or alcohol/drug abuse), but the rates are much lower for kids of authoritative parents.

Under this approach, which is also sometimes referred to as inductive discipline approach, a parent takes time to explain to the child that a certain behavior needs to be changed, and the change will have certain specific affects on others. This also helps develop the child's empathy skills by seeing behavior may affect the lives specific other people. Research has shown that the more frequently inductive discipline is used at home, the less frequently children engaged in disruptive behavior in school.

To the little girl who forgot to put away her shoes, the authoritative parent will listen to the explanation about the restroom exigency and provide empathy. "Wow, you must have been really holding it in and had to go pretty badly. Sounds like you were in quite a rush. Well, I'm glad you made it to the latrine in time. But we still have the problem with the shoes out of place. I could have tripped on them and hurt myself. Our home looks a bit untidy now. And we both have to take time away from play in order to address it. Since this cost us some time, I'll need to take away fifteen minutes of screen time from you today, but hopefully it won't happen again."

IN SUMMARY

Parenting style has a major influence on how the child is raised. While there are numerous approaches to parenting, the authoritative approach tends to work best for children. It involves a high level of warmth in administering consequences, coupled with simple explanations of the rules, and the effects certain actions will have on others.

CHAPTER 10:
"POTTY" TRAINING

There are a number of approaches available to parents "potty training." The average age that children are encouraged to leave the diaper behind and use the latrine is between two to three years, although some parents have reported the behavior as early as seven months. Generally, however, early age success may be more elusive, because a child won't be physically capable of "holding it" until the muscles required to "hold it" have sufficiently developed.

When the time arrives for "potty training," parents have a number of options for which method to employ. Generally, however, parents should avoid methods that involve yelling and threatening. Perhaps the most effective method may be the weekend intensive approach. This may take place over a single weekend, although it is best if done over a two-week period, ideally corresponding with some holiday during which both parents are home and able to assist one another. Below is a brief summary of this approach:

- **Pot**: Have a small pot at the ready at all times. If parents are expected to travel during this period, then a portable pot should be packed. Parents should not go anywhere for the two-week period without the portable pot.

- **Rewards**: Parents will need to use a rewards system, employing small toys and stickers. The toys can be wrapped up as small presents and placed in a box from which the child can choose. After each successful potty trip, the child can choose one reward. Food should not be used as a reward system, as it can lead to harmful eating habits and unwanted emotional food attachment.

- **Big Deal**: After each successful potty trip, parents should make a big deal out of it, perhaps jumping up and down, clapping, and recruiting others in the household to do the same. Parents can also place a telephone call to someone, a grandparent or aunt or uncle, and then allow the child to brag about the accomplishment. This will reinforce the positive experience and encourage the child to try again on the pot.

- For little boys, parents may place Cheerios or other store bought target floaties into the toilet for aiming, which may help create an incentive to "hold it" until they can play the game.

- As food and water intake is closely monitored, parents should place the child on the toilet or pot at regular intervals. There should be plenty of books near the pot to occupy the waiting period. Parents are encouraged to buy new books for this activity so that the child has something new to look forward to.

IN SUMMARY

While it would be great to leave the diapers behind, children may simply not be physically able to control when and where they go until the requisite muscles have developed. This may have to wait until they are two or three years old. When the time comes, parents should employ one of many methods available, but care should be taken to avoid intimidation or fear tactics, and food should not be used as a reward system.

CHAPTER 11:
HEALTHY EATING

As the child grows and matures, choosing the right foods will be paramount to proper development. Not only does good nutrition provide the essential building blocks for a growing child's body, it will also replenish the quickly draining energy supplies of the active child who is constantly expending energy at rates on par with Olympic athletes. Parents will inevitably face numerous challenges as they strive to provide adequate and proper nutritious foods for the child. There will be obstacles placed before them by the chaos of frazzled lives limited by time constraints, which will in turn be compounded by the daily struggles of the child's eventual refusal to eat certain foods as she morphs into what has been referred to in the civilian sector as a "picky eater." But it is essential for parents to ensure that the growing child gets the requisite food supply for its current needs while simultaneously developing healthy eating habits to carry into adulthood.

Research has shown that a child has certain food preferences long before ever tasting any solid foods. These early predilections are a result of her genetic code as well as the diet of the pregnant or breastfeeding mother. In one study, a drop of sugar water produced a smile and a happy baby, but a drop of bitter liquid got a visible negative reaction. This, of course, has evolutionary justifications as sugar is the very energy source a child needs to grow and flourish, while bitterness is often associated with poisonous foods.

AVOIDING METABOLIC SYNDROME

According to the American Heart Association, the Metabolic Syndrome, MetSyn, is a "cluster of metabolic disorders" that can lead to large increases in the chances of getting cardiovascular disease (such as heart attack or stroke), Type-2 diabetes, and premature mortality. Indeed, MetSyn affects a large percentage of the American population, and is often referred to as the "American Syndrome," although by no means is it limited to America. It is not a disease in and of itself, but serves as a major indicator of an individual's potentially fatal medical future. It is generally understood that a person has MetSyn if any three or more of the following conditions are present:

- Abdominal obesity;

- High blood pressure;

- High blood sugar;

- High serum triglycerides; and

- Low high-density lipoproteins (HDL).

The human body thrives and gets stronger when it receives the proper proportions of the proper building blocks. These same building blocks also serve as energy sources to enable the body to do all that it does. Modern practices have unfortunately transformed human society into a culture of excess, and as a result, humans consume food in obscene amounts with the inevitable corollary of an unhealthy body.

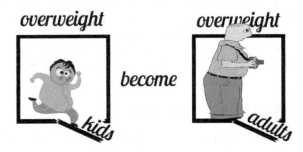

Children thrive when parents are around to provide nurturing, supervision, and general guidance in life. But in order to accomplish this, parents need to stick around as long as possible. If parents succumb to premature mortality, especially as a result of preventable causes such as MetSyn, it can have tectonic consequences for the child for the remainder of his or her life. Therefore, not only should parents strive to keep children as healthy and thriving as possible, but they should also work hard on themselves and their own health. If a parental unit knowingly and voluntarily exposes itself to premature death (excess and poor food choices, inadequate exercise, and so on), the message to the child is not necessarily one of love. Luckily, making good choices is usually within the control of most humans. Below are tactics parents should employ to protect the child against the pernicious effects of MetSyn:

- **Reduce Hypertension**. Reduce salt intake. For the adults, reduce alcohol and caffeine. Reduce red meat, but increase fish consumption. Exercise regularly.

- **Manage Obesity**. There are two main types - belly fat and generalized fat—under the skin, everywhere. The former (belly fat) is primarily caused by fructose intake, and may be the more lethal of the two. Parents are encouraged to modify caloric intake and caloric burn by reducing the amounts consumed and increasing the amounts burned through regular exercise.

- **Dramatically Reduce Sugar**: Reduce or eliminate sweets entirely. Eliminate all sugary drinks, especially juice, even the "organic" and "freshly squeezed" kinds. The Vitamin C contained in these juices is overshadowed by the pernicious effects of the fructose. As our understanding and knowledge about sugar and its harmful effects grows, it is only an uninformed doctor that will still instruct a parent to give a child juice (even the diluted kinds). One glass of juice typically contains the same amount of fructose as a can of soda. Don't be fooled by labels that tout "No High Fructose Corn Syrup" as science is learning that it is the actual *amounts* of fructose, stripped of its meaty pulp, which has us consuming more fruit sugar than our bodies have ever seen in the history of our species. Once sugar is reduced, one should also reduce the intake of carbohydrate (breads, pastas, cereals) from the diet. These are metabolically just one single step away from being broken down into sugar. Have an overall increase in fiber consumption. Same for protein; and exercise more.

- **Modify What/When To Eat**. Also, change the actual process of eating. Eat until "no longer hungry" (rather than until "full"). As there is a slight temporal delay between the time the stomach is actually full and the brain finding out about it, this will allow that message of, "I no longer need food" sufficient time to reach its destination. Eat slowly. Bigger breakfasts, smaller lunches, and smallest dinners, increasing the protein intake as the day wears on, and consuming most of the carbohydrates (breads, pastas, cereals) earlier in the day.

- **Manage Heart Disease**. High Triglycerides, High LDL, Low HDL. Eliminate trans fats (fried foods, fast food). Replace saturated fats (sausage, bacon, eggs, chocolate, cheese, milk) with unsaturated fats. Unsaturated fats fall into two main categories: poly-unsaturated fats and mono-unsaturated fats. Increase mono-unsaturated fats by consuming more nuts, avocados, and olive oil. Increase poly-unsaturated fats by consuming sunflower seeds, vegetable oils, a handful of nuts (of all kinds) per day, and Coldwater fish (herring, tuna, salmon, mackerel).

- **Exercise, Exercise, Exercise**. For each of the metabolic syndrome categories, exercise is recommended in high dosages. Getting the body to move and burn away all of the excess poisons that have accumulated go a long way in keeping both the parent and the child alive and thriving for a long time.

ADDITIONAL TIPS

Below are some additional tips to help bring the family in line with proper nutrition needs.

- **Water**. Millions of years ago, we humans left the oceans for dry land, but arguably we never truly left the oceans behind. We carry water with us in our bodies. The human body is composed mostly of water that is essential for life. A human body can survive days, perhaps weeks without food, but not without water. Water serves many purposes. It cools the body, serves as the body's river and helps deliver energy and nutrients to remote cells, lubricates the joints, and moistens the parts of the body like the eyes, lips, and so on. Parents are encouraged to offer plenty of water throughout the day to the child. A good measure of whether there is sufficient water in the system is to observe the color of urine. If it is a dark yellow, the body needs water right away. Ideally, you should strive for a pale yellow or even clear color. Avoid the temptation to give sports drinks or juices after heavy exertion. The sugar is poisonous and unless the child is an Olympic athlete, there is nothing that the sports drink can offer that water and some fruit won't do.

- **Sometimes Foods.** It is almost axiomatic that depriving a human of a certain thing will only lead to an increased desire for it. If you tell the child she can't have gum, then that will only make the gum more coveted, and will likely lead the child to find a way to have gum when not in the presence of the parent. To combat this, a good strategy that parents can adopt is the concept of "sometimes foods." The child is encouraged to do his or her best to avoid the foods that can lead to MetSyn. However, create pressure valves for the child to experience those foods. Make them "*sometimes* foods." Allow them to have candy or juice, for example, at birthday parties or trips to amusement parks. Perhaps allow the child to consume juice when they have a cold or the flu, which can also help increase fluid intake. Create one day a week to go out as a family and have ice cream together. This reinforces the idea that these foods are not good for you when consumed on a regular basis, but acknowledges that they are certainly delicious and every now and then may not be so bad.

- **Early Exposure to Healthy Foods.** The foods a mother eats while pregnant will influence the child's taste preferences. In one particular experiment, mothers were put into three groups. In the first group, mothers ate a lot of carrots during pregnancy; in the second group, a lot of carrots while breastfeeding; and in the third group, the mothers did not eat any carrots at all. The children who had been exposed to carrots either during pregnancy or breastfeeding were significantly more likely to eat carrots when they finally started eating solid foods. Pregnant or breastfeeding mothers are thereby encouraged to eat a lot of healthy foods and on a regular basis. This will increase the likelihood of the child acquiring healthy eating habits when they grow older. Conversely, avoid eating fatty and sugary foods, as it will be more difficult to wean the child off of it.

PICKY EATERS

As the child becomes mobile, and much to the parents' chagrin, the now crawling child will be a voracious and indiscriminate eater, putting just about anything into his or her mouth. However, something happens around age two, and children become hyper-selective about what they eat, accepting only a few familiar foods and rejecting everything else. This behavior may be best explained as a survival tactic of human evolution. At around the age of two, historically a newly mobile cave-child living in the forest and wandering away from the protective presence of its parents would have found itself exposed to foods that could potentially be poisonous. As such, the child suddenly develops an aversion for everything but the safest and most familiar foods, and only through time and extreme caution will it even consider any new foods. Studies have, to a large extent, proven this to be true and children will eventually, after repeated exposure, accept new foods.

Below are some tips on dealing with a picky eater:

- **Repeated exposure**. Parents are encouraged to expose the child to new foods repeatedly. Attempt to get the child to at least try a small amount of everything that you present. The child's body will process the foods and find it safe. Repeating such exposure to the food will eventually lead to the child coming back for more. The human body knows what is good for it and often develops a craving for food that it finds nutritious. It may take up to fifteen false starts, but eventually, the child should accept the food.

- **Combine**. To aid in a child's acceptance of new foods, parents should strive to combine the new food with something that the child already likes, such as chopping up a bell pepper into their favorite egg sandwich. This will make it more palatable and easier to adopt.

- **Hunger**. Research has shown that when the body is hungry, it will often crave any food. This hunger craving provides a doorway for parents to introduce new foods. When introducing something new, do not do so after the child has just eaten a hearty meal or filled themselves with snacks or other foods. Wait until hunger has set in, and then introduce the new food, and as with the previous tip, combine it with something familiar that the child already likes.

- **Modeling Good Food**. A very strong predictor of the food choices children will adopt is based on what kind of foods the parents consume. Research has shown that children will increase their own consumption of fruits and vegetables to mirror that of their parents. Therefore, parents are encouraged to adopt a healthy eating lifestyle as soon as possible using the guidelines contained herein. Doing so has the added benefit of a healthy parent. In making these healthy choices, parents should eat healthy foods and exercise in front of the children so that they see.

Below are a few things that parents should avoid when trying to get the picky eater to choose new foods:

- **New Foods During Illness**. Just as research suggests combining new foods with familiar foods may increase the likelihood of accepting new foods, conversely, associating new foods with certain negative things may discourage adopting of the new food. For starters, parents should avoid introducing a new food when the child is ill. The body instinctively will keep tabs on foods that have proven to be poisonous, and it will assume this new food is what was responsible. Rat experiments have shown that giving a rat a novel food while it is ill will result in the rat avoiding that particular food for the rest of its life. This may be the very reason most adults dislike certain foods -- they ate it as a child when they were ill.

- **No Need To Try A Lot**. In addition to avoiding presenting new foods while ill, parents should avoid pressuring the child to eat large quantities of a novel food. The approach is a gentle but firm encouragement to try a small quantity of the novel food, and then come back to it another time.

- **No Coercion**. Connected to the previous tip, parents should also avoid coercive methods in getting the child to try new foods. This will ultimately create a negative association with the food similar to trying too much of it or trying it during an illness, thereby reducing the chances of the food being adopted as part of a diet.

Parents are encouraged to be patient and allow nature to do its work. While initially resistant, the child's own natural system will eventually do its job.

IN SUM

While a lot of factors can affect a child's development, few things are as important as food. Below are things to remember:

- Parents should be mindful of the metabolic syndrome and reduce sugars and other bad foods

- Children (and parents) should exercise more

- Parents should also adopt healthy life styles

- Encourage kids to drink lots of water, but avoid juices and other sugary drinks

- To avoid a backlash, offer sweets as "sometimes foods"

- Expose children to healthy foods early, and frequently

- In dealing with a picky eater, combine foods with accepted foods, introduce new foods while the child is hungry, and avoid doing so when the child is under the weather.

CHAPTER 12:
SICK TIME

No matter how many healthy meals parents pack and how much exercise the child gets, inevitably a time will come when children succumb to the brigades of germs that have them constantly under siege. In this section, parents will learn various strategies to minimize the chances for some of the more common ailments such as the cold and the flu, as well as suggestions on what to do once the child has fallen ill. At every step along the way, parents should be in constant communication with the unit physician to ensure proper procedures are being followed for their individual family. Above all, the child will require a bit more love and care during this period, so parents should be prepared for extra hugs and kisses (preferably with a mask to protect the parent and avoid the endless volley of germs back and forth).

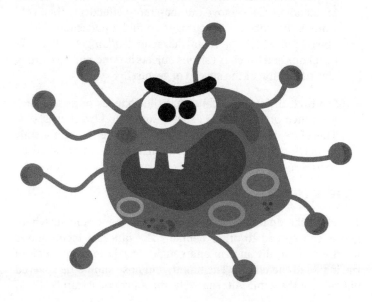

AVOID

The best approach is to try to ward off an illness. As germs surround the child, her personal defenses need to be fortified. While by no means exhaustive, below is a list of some of the more common methods to aid in prevention:

- **Washing hands**. As children navigate the day, they will constantly come into contact with germs from all directions. People that are infected touch doorknobs, toys, cups, chairs, or any other surface within reach. By touching an infected surface, children will contract those germs. One of the best tools to prevent this is to try to get children into the habit of regularly washing hands. Hands should be washed with soap, warm water, and the soap should be rubbed in for at least 20 seconds (this is roughly the time it takes to sing the "ABC Song" once through). Parents should supervise the initial few attempts at hand washing and teach the proper method of wetting the hands, applying soap, rubbing it on the whole hand, forward and backwards, between the fingers, and then rinsing with warm water (which is able to break down and remove the soap more effectively than cold water). Parents are encouraged to find a particular *Caillou* episode in which the main character *Caillou* gets glitter on his hands and touches various objects around him, providing a visualization of the spread of germs.

- **Contact**. Inform the child that the chances of getting sick are much greater when around someone else that is sick. Therefore, it is best to steer clear of people that are visibly displaying signs of illness. Coughing, sneezing, and increased irritation are the general signs to have the child look for.

PROPER COUGH/SNEEZE

The child should be taught to avoid coughing into the air where germs can spread to other people. The quickest technique is for the child to lift an arm and cough directly into the nook of the inside of the elbow. The mouth and nose should be covered entirely by the arm. Alternatively, the shirt collar can be lifted and the cough can be done inside the shirt. Parents should look for short educational videos on the web to let the child get a visual of the sneeze or the cough.

ADEQUATE SLEEP

Children should get adequate sleep based on the recommended sleep amounts for their particular age. If the child does get sick, plan for an increased amount of sleep to allow the body to fight off the foreign invaders.

HYDRATION

Perhaps the most important weapon in the child's arsenal against illness is water. Parents should give the child as much water as necessary to transform the urine into a clear color. When the body is sick, its need for hydration is increased, and the child will need to be encouraged to drink more throughout the day. While the normal response is to avoid sugary drinks, a lightly diluted juice/water mixture can help the child drink more fluids during a bout with the cold or flu. When giving fluids, fill the glass only to the point where the child can finish all of it. This will allow the parent to adequately measure the intake of fluids and give the child a sense of accomplishment. Water bottles are more difficult to drink from. Fluids should be close to **room temperature** to increase consumption, since chilled water goes down slower. Chicken soup is an excellent source of hydration and also provides lots of other nutrients (discussed below) that the body will need to recuperate.

FRUITS/VEGETABLES

Consumption of fruits and vegetables should be increased during periods of germ invasions to help the body strengthen its defenses. Finding fruits such as citrus that have an increased the amount of Vitamin C can help shorten the length of the infection. Chicken soup can provide an excellent source of hydration, as well as other nutrients, to help in the recovery.

MEDICINES

If there is a fever, parents should have on hand their doctor's recommended pain and fever medication. If the child is coughing excessively, medication may be considered, but this should be in close consultation with the physician as certain cough medicines are not recommended for younger children. A spoonful of honey can go a long ways in soothing a sore throat and a cough. There are also honey-based medicines that can help sooth the coughing. Rubbing the child's chest with some Vick's Vapor Rub has also been shown to be effective in the reduction of the coughing and aiding in sleep.

EQUIPMENT

The room in which the child sleeps should have a humidifier on throughout the night. This will help suppress congestion and also help with the cough. A thermometer should be easily accessible to quickly monitor and report to the doctor unusual temperatures. A sound machine will also help the child sleep easily throughout the night.

ACTIVITIES

Being knocked down with the cold or flu is going to be no fun for the child, and parents should try to alleviate the discomfort. Below are some suggestions:

- **Avoid Strenuous Activities**. The child should avoid strenuous activity and rest as often as possible during this period. In order to help in this, parents should avoid outdoor activity to the extent possible and stick to relaxing indoor games.

- **Indoor Activities**. Floor puzzles are great, as are board games such as "Chutes and Ladders" and various "Memory" or matching games. In addition, playing with blocks, Legos, painting, and coloring are all excellent activities to keep the child entertained while letting the body do its restorative work.

- **Reading**. Parents should have plenty of books and kids magazines on hand for the child to read or be read to. Please refer to the chapter of book lists and movie lists for a good resource.

CHAPTER 13:
LANGUAGE

Children have both a need and an ability to communicate from the very first day of arrival. Lacking any other means of communication, especially to express unhappiness or discomfort, crying is initially the sole means of getting its point across. In those early days, the newborn needs to be able to let the parent know when it is hungry, tired, in pain, or simply in need of a diaper change. Using these needs as a checklist, parents can often quickly discern the cause of those predawn piercing sounds.

As the child grows, an enormous amount of learning takes place, and language can get a big boost from the child's interactions with parents. Often by the third month, the infant has become sufficiently familiar with certain voices and will turn towards them while also making cooing sounds. Another three or four months and she will recognize her own name. By nine months, she may also be able to understand a few words. As early as twelve months, she may enter into the world of spoken language and utter her first word, often a simple noun, with verbs not following for another few months.

SIGN LANGUAGE

In those early months, and while the vocal skills have not fully developed yet, the infant does actually have the ability to communicate beyond the initial cries. Parents are encouraged to teach basic sign language to the child beginning at around four months, allowing the child to both receive and send messages. This will not only bring a level of happiness to the child as he/she gains the satisfaction of getting their point across, but it will also provide fun interaction between parent and child. Using sign language can also promote language development and a number of cognitive tests have shown improved scores with children who have learned sign. The actual instruction does not need to be formal, and parents can come up with their own symbols to represent simple concepts such as "milk," "more," and "diaper change."

Some parents may be hesitant to teach sign fearing that it may hinder the child's normal speech development and delay her first words. To explore this concern, research was undertaken and the results were clear: not only does it not hinder normal speech development, but also children may indeed have learned to speak earlier than those who did not use sign language.

PARENTESE

In those initial months and years, parents and other family members are encouraged to provide as much of language stimulation as possible. Parents should talk to the infant from birth, and using the same or similar words as speaking to an older child, or even an adult. Indeed, parents should engage often in "child directed" conversation, speaking to the child as if to an adult and often allowing the child's responses to affect and modify what the parent is doing. Parents may, for example, simply have a conversation about the day they have had.

Research has shown that adults will often modify their voice in speaking to infants, taking on a sing-song tone where the words are spoken slower, but in a lyrical fashion, and vocabulary is slowed and vowels are extended. This is often referred to as "motherese" or "fatherese" or simply "parentese." It has been shown that if children are taught certain new words in this parentese, they are significantly more likely to retain that information.

No Baby Talk

With that said, parents should avoid using "baby talk" where certain nonsense words are used to describe simple things, such as "num-num" to describe food or "owee" to describe pain or injury.

SECOND LANGUAGE

There is a growing body of evidence supporting the incredible cognitive benefits of acquiring a second language during early childhood. It can lead to improvements in memory, creativity, reading comprehension, and flexible problem solving skills. Some research has pointed to the fact that children who grow up bilingual may even have a later onset of dementia, delayed even more if the child was trilingual. Parents need not be concerned that the child may not speak a language other than their primary language. The evidence suggests that even small exposure to and usage of a second language can prove beneficial to the child. While most American families only speak one language, most of the countries around the world are bilingual, which may partially explain the education deficit American school children face when compared to the rest of the world.

The exact reasons for these benefits are still being explored, but some hypotheses include the concept that a second language improves the brain activation of the child, thereby increasing its neuronal connections. A bilingual child may simply have a more densely connected brain. There has also been evidence that bilingual kids have a slightly bigger inferior frontal cortex, especially if the bilingual child is engaged in reading activities.

Parents have several options available to provide a second language training program for children, all of which ideally should be explored before the age of 12, as research suggests children may be able to learn new languages with less instruction than after the age of 12.

Schools: For starters, there is an increasing number of schools around the country that offer a second language curriculum, even as early as elementary school. These can serve as an excellent opportunity for second languages, and if available, parents should enroll their children into such a school. If local schools do not offer such a program, a petition from enough parents may be sufficient to press upon current schools to take some action because of the importance of a second language.

E-Help: If second languages schools are not an option, parents should not despair. There are a number of smartphone and tablet applications that are also effective in setting the stage for more advanced language instructions later. Some of these apps have a fairly simple curriculum requiring as little as five minutes a day of activities in order to see results.

Immersion: Language immersion would always be the most optimal choice, and if the family has a particular member who is fluent in a particular language other than English, it may be beneficial to request that they provide a weekly language class. Parents can also request of that particular relative to speak to the child strictly in the foreign language. If feasible for the family, taking the child on a month long trip to a foreign land may offer an enormous amount of benefit, as such a deep level of immersion may be precisely what will make the child fluent.

READING

Reading is demonstrably one of the most important steps of human evolutionary advancement, and its influence on children is no less important. Early exposure to reading is strongly correlated with a later love for reading as well as reading mastery later in school. Parents are therefore encouraged to give children exposure to reading as early as when they are infants.

Nightly Routine and Book Selection

Part of the benefit of reading is the simple joy that begins to be associated with the activity of sitting with parents every night as a routine before bed. Parents can enhance this joy of reading by allowing the child to choose which books to read. At an earlier age, and much to the parents' chagrin, the child may end up choosing the same two or three books night after night. While cumbersome to the parents, this is perfectly normal for the child, since they may see things with each subsequent read that they will have missed in previous readings. They also become more familiar with certain words, and the rhyming structure, which may be evident to the parent at first read but not become evident to the child until perhaps the twentieth reading. Encourage the child to choose whichever book she wants, and to approach the reading with a joyful approach. Encourage the child to read, but parents should avoid pushing the child too much. Avoid at all times linking reading with any sort of punishment, which can create negative associations. However, the taking *away* of reading as a form of consequence for negative behavior may actually create a stronger positive association with the child (we covet what we cannot have).

Plain and Simple Books

While store shelves may be filled with gimmicky noisy books, research has demonstrated that simple books with simple pictures and words are better for the learning child. While children may certainly enjoy the sounds and the pop up effects of the loud books, children may actually learn more from less. Therefore when presenting book options, parents should stick to the "less is more" approach and purchase more traditional books.

- A great example is the old book, "Goodnight Moon."

- Once the child shows signs of starting to read, an excellent series of books is the "Bob Books" series offering various levels that can help facilitate the child's next steps into reading.

Outside World

As the child becomes familiar with words, parents should practice reading with the child throughout the day and wherever they are. Point out signs on the streets or in stores and show to the child that reading can help unlock many of the mysteries of the world in which it finds itself.

Into the Teen Years

Parents should not stop reading to older children, as there is research to suggest its benefits for children as old as fourteen. By hearing a more experienced adult read words and sentences, they get a better understanding of how to put words together and where to place emphasis in certain phrases.

CHAPTER 14:
EDUCATION

By the fourth year of a child's life, children will usually require some level of outside education, and parents will have to select a school system in which to enroll the child. This process can begin as early as the daycare stage and eventually go on beyond high school into the selection process involved in graduate school. In this chapter, parents will be given general guidance on school selection, homework regulation, tips on scholastic success, and a few basic guidelines on preparing for education beyond high school.

MONTESSORI SCHOOLS

Maria Montessori was a groundbreaking teacher who helped revolutionize the human education process. Her methods focus on children's interactions with real world material to help enhance learning. Parents have seen a tremendous benefit from her methodology. There is currently likely a Montessori school in nearly every city in America.

It should be noted that there is no central Montessori certification system for schools, and there is no minimum standard requirements to have the name "Montessori" attached to a school, so parents are encouraged to spend some time learning the Montessori methodology and then inquire of the potential school how closely they adhere to that methodology. Look for schools with smaller classes, as research points to major benefits with a smaller teacher/student ratio.

Home Like School

While parents should select Montessori schools when looking for outside instruction, the home environment should also attempt to reflect a typical Montessori classroom.

Update Material

Children should be provided with material that is appropriate for their level of development. Over time, as the child grows and develops, the material should be modified to keep pace with that change. Parents should add some things and take away other things to make the necessary adjustments. Regardless of how great one particular object may be, children will inevitably exhaust its interesting aspects over time.

Simple Uncluttered Room

The child's room should be calming and colorful, containing child sized furniture.

- Parents should keep flashy electronics out of the room, including televisions and computers. There should also be few stuffed animals to minimize overall distraction.

- And as for the walls, while not bare, should be simple and fairly muted in order not to distract the child from what it is doing.

- The environment in which the child lives and thrives should be orderly, clean, and uncluttered.

- Shelves are not packed, but neat and objects are spaced out from one another. When new things are added, other things are taken away so as to maintain uncluttered order. When a child takes something to play with, there should be a clear gap left so that they know where to return the object once play is done.

- Parents are encouraged to give the child a level of responsibility in maintaining order in their environment.

The child should be permitted to explore the environment freely, limited solely by her own curiosity.

MATH, THE "VILLAIN"

American society has shifted its relationship to math, and most discussions regarding any mathematics involve at least some level of vilification of the subject. In fact, nearly every reference to math in the media is negative. Negative phrases such as, "I am bad at math" and, "Math is hard," and, "I never liked math" are commonplace in film and television and get engrained in adults. Parents often pass down these negative attitudes to their children. Research has shown that a negative attitude towards math does indeed lead to lower test results, and this is *especially pronounced in girls*.

Parents are encouraged to break this chain and stop making negative references in regards to mathematics. While it is not an easy subject, like many other things, navigating it depends on proper instruction and lots of practice. By removing the aversion to it, parents can encourage the child to stick with it, particularly later on with longer math concepts that may require sustained effort. American students are not leading in mathematics aptitude tests in some part at least because of this negative attitude towards the subject.

Parents should find hope that success in math in the early years has been linked to many benefits later in life. Children who score higher in math and have a better understanding of numbers generally are more like to start and graduate from college. Math proficiency is significantly related to better employment and average annual salary. Proficiency in math doesn't only get good grades, but ultimately will pay for a better life.

COUNTING CHAINS, THE 100-BOARD, AND THE DIVISION BOARD

Children who acquire a certain "number sense" early in life will see success with mathematics later. This number sense can be taught. There are a number of supplies that can be purchased from a variety of outlets that can help the child prepare for the scholastic lessons that lie ahead in school. Parents should get simple boards such as the "100-Board" that give the child a visual understanding of numbers. This will place the value of numbers onto a visible and tangible object, thereby allowing the child to truly understand what counting by ten, for example, is.

Along with the 100-Board, children should be presented with various board games that call for counting spaces. In particular, the traditional game "Chutes and Ladders" does the very thing that the 100-Board does by presenting a field of 100 squares through which the player must navigate. Play this game and play it often with the child. There is a lot of research that connects board game experience with better math skills.

One of the basic supply items found at a most true Montessori schools is called "Counting Chains." Parents are encouraged to buy or make these chains to help the child gain an early mastery of and a much deeper understanding of numbers than they would otherwise get from rote memorization. These chains can initially help teach counting, but the learning complexity can be gradually increased to help the child learn addition, multiplication, square numbers, and even cubes.

Browsing an online Montessori catalog such as that offered by Lakeshore can give parents other ideas to use for inspiration in making do-it-yourself homemade materials.

FRACTIONS

By the age of ten, most children have gotten the fundamentals down and are preparing for the many challenging years of mathematics ahead. Interestingly enough, mastery of fractions has been shown to make the upcoming challenges of math much easier to handle. While the research looked at various different math skills and aptitude test scores, the strongest correlation involved a mastery of fractions. Therefore, it is imperative that children have a strong sense of fractions by age ten.

Parents are encouraged to work with the child to boost an understanding and proficiency of fractions. There are a number of workbooks available for purchase. In addition, parents can discuss with the child's teachers the extent fractions are being taught in the classroom and what can be done to increase that instruction. Also, parents can speak regularly with the child about fractions throughout the day by pointing out real-world scenarios in which fractions become relevant. A simple example is distributing four cookies between two children.

HOMEWORK

While a great deal of instruction takes place in the classroom, research has found a strong correlation between the amount of time spent on homework and the level of academic achievement. Homework enhances and reinforces classroom instruction, preparing the child for the next level of instruction, which in turn builds on what was previously learned. There are a number of steps parents can take to help the child succeed in the classroom by enhancing the amount and quality of time spent on homework. Studies have shown that following the below guidelines has led not only to greater academic achievement, but also less arguments with parents about homework.

11. Share Research: For starters, parents are encouraged to share with the child the results of the research connecting schoolwork and homework. Explain to the child that proper homework will not only increase learning, but will help the child score better on tests and exams.

12. **Procedure - Time (Involve Child)**: Parents should make it clear that there will be a daily carved out period known as "learning time" or "study time" during which the child will do some deliberate learning, even if no homework has been assigned by the school. To do this, and it is important that it is in consultation with the child, parents should establish a consistent time during which there will be no other distractions. This time may be immediately upon arrival to the home from school or after dinner time, but whatever time is chosen, the child should be involved in the decision making, thereby empowering the child in the process and allowing him/her to have a certain ownership of the activity. Avoid making this period too close to bedtime, as not only will this deprive the child of the proper amount of sleep, but there is ample evidence that concentration levels drop dramatically close to bedtime after a long and likely eventful day.

13. **Procedure - Place (Involve Child)**: Along with a set time, parents, again in consultation with the child, should designate a consistent place for learning time. This can be done at the kitchen table, provided there won't be other distractions such as siblings running around or a television blaring in the background. This can also be in the bedroom. While place consistency is generally encouraged, parents should strive to break the routine occasionally to allow for the child to study in different environments –a practice linked to better achievement.

14. **10-Minute Rule**: Under the "10-minute rule," the amount of time that the child should spend on homework on any given day should correspond to ten minutes for every grade. So, for example, a second grader should spend twenty minutes on homework, a fourth grader forty, a sixth grader an hour, and a senior two hours. Working on homework for longer

than this often leads to burnout, and corresponds to actually lower levels of academic achievement.

PARENT HELP WITH HOMEWORK

There is a strong negative correlation between the amount of help a parent gives a student on certain material and student performance on exams. The more time the student puts into the homework on his or her own, the better the score. The takeaway here is that the child should be allowed to work independently and put in a serious effort to get to the solution of problems.

There will, however, be times when a parent will need to step in and help on a topic with which the child is struggling. When doing so, parents are encouraged to follow a specific method of helping known as the theory of "scaffolding." Under this method, parents should offer as little help as possible to keep the child going. When working through a math problem, for example, and a mistake is spotted, the parent should not correct the mistake; instead, the parent should ask to be walked through the process the child used to get the answer, with the hopes that together they will identify the misstep along the way. When the next time help is required on a similar problem, the support provided should be a little less, allowing the child to work through more of it on her own. What is important is not a completed assignment, but that the child worked through the problems and learned in the process.

BREAKS/SPACING

Breaks: Research has shown that learning increases when students are able to take breaks during the learning period. For a two-hour study period, the child absorbs more if the period is divided into two one-hour sessions, separated by a break in between. Indeed, if divided into four half-hour sessions, there is even more learning. Parents are thus encouraged to space out the study sessions such that there is a break for every 20-30 minutes of study time. This will enable greater learning and prevent brain fatigue.

Rotate (If Can't Break): If, however, due to the exigencies of the night, there is no time for breaks, the child should rotate the subject that they work on. For example, the first twenty minutes of the study period should be on mathematics, followed by twenty minutes of language arts, and so on. This way, no one topic will lead to brain fatigue, and the brain is constantly changing gears and learning something new.

MEMORY ENHANCEMENT

The human brain functions on both short and long-term memory. With short-term memory, we focus attention on whatever information is received through sensory input. This memory is usually evanescent and stored for a very brief period, serving us just long enough to work through our physical environment. This is also known as "working memory." In order to retain any of this information for more permanent keeping, it needs to be transferred to "long-term memory."

Traditionally, a display of creativity and scores on aptitude tests have been good predictors of how the child will do later in school, but memory and retention is often a better predictor. On a test known as the Digital Span Memory Task, researchers read a set of digits to the subject and asked the subject to recall the digits. Younger children will only be able to recite two to three digits, but as the child gets older, the number increases to what is typical for an adult—seven digits. This test has been a better predictor of school success than most other tests. Below are some techniques that parents can employ to improve children's memory:

- **Memory Games**. Certain memory games tend to have positive effects on long-term memory transition. Perhaps throughout the day, parents can present the child with a particular set of instructions to follow. Once those instructions are mastered, the chain of instructions is increased, forcing the child to memorize the list in order to follow it. Another excellent game is the traditional "Memory" game of matching in which players take turns flipping two cards at a time in order to find a match.

- **Rehearsal**. One of the simplest and earliest techniques that the child can employ actively to retain particular information is to practice rehearsal. Like an actor memorizing script lines, it merely requires repeating something over and over until it gains more permanence. If, for example, the child is trying to remember a phone number, it would be repeated over and over until it is remembered. Parents are encouraged to teach this sometime around four or five years of age.

- **Visualizations**.   Another simple method to transition information into long-term memory is through visualization. The human brain seems to be adapted to retrieve visual images much better than hard facts, as evidenced by the ability to remember what the rooms of a childhood home looked like, but not the physical address.   While some children will learn this technique on their own, encourage them to practice it in a variety of situations. Most people may have trouble finding the various countries on a map, but not many have any difficulty finding the boot in Europe that is Italy. The child can begin to employ this technique sometime in early elementary school at around the age of eight or nine.

- **Mnemonics**.   An excellent but slightly more advanced technique is to employ mnemonics to organize information. Taking the example of the names and order of the planets in our own solar system, the child would remember something like, "My Very Eager Mother Just Served Us Nectarines" to give, in order, Mercury, Venus, Earth, Mars, Jupiter, Saturn, Uranus, and Neptune (the status of poor Pluto is still in flux, as she has, of course, been released recently with an honorable discharge). Parents can begin to teach this technique as the child reaches the age of nine or ten.

- **Chunking**.   Similar to the mnemonic method, chunking involves organizing information in a familiar manner. Humans employ chunking all of the time, particularly in reading. Letters are chunked into groups, called words, and they help make sense of the characters on the page. Similarly, in memorizing a phone number, the numbers are often chunked into three groups of 3-3-4.

- **More**.   These memory-enhancing techniques are by no
  means exhaustive. Parents are encouraged to research other
  techniques, preferably with the child's help, and adapt them
  to the current task at hand.

HIGHER EDUCATION

At some point, parents will set their sights on higher education
for the child, and begin the process of preparing, both in terms of
the cost and the selection of higher education. While it is one of
the most important investments people can make in their lives,
the college preparation process can be daunting. Often, students
choose the wrong major, the wrong school, the wrong source of
financing, or merely the wrong decision on whether to attend
college in the first place.

Major: First, some basic research on the subject. There is
strong evidence that the choice of major is far more predicative
of financial success than the actual school attended. The more
specialized the major, the higher correlation that the profession
chosen will be in that specialized major. The payoff is higher
when the student invests in a specialized major, particularly in

a high demand field. For example, there may be a higher pay out for engineering majors than for the more generalized psychology majors. This is not to say that enjoying your chosen profession is not important. Research shows that beyond a certain base point of income, happiness becomes dependent on enjoying the day-to-day experience of the profession itself.

Preparation: A good predictor of success is having strong skills in processing new and complex information, and also possessing the ability to complete high-quality written material. These skills generally tend to funnel the student into more prestigious institutions, and into more specialized or high-demand fields.

Planning the Cost: The cost of education can be staggering, and by the time today's child is in school, the cost may have doubled or even tripled. Most people will likely have to borrow money to go to college, and if there is a lower likelihood of graduation, or a field is chosen that will not reward with a higher salary, the cost of attending college becomes a fairly large risk with a colossal loan dangling over the graduate's head. It is important to begin early to foster the skills necessary to prepare the child for future success, but also to put in place the financial resources to supplement the high costs. There are various tax incentives to encourage parents to do this early. The main vehicle is the "**529**" plan, which permits tax-free withdrawals provided the money is used for qualified educational purposes. While the contribution itself is not a tax deduction, any capital gains would be if used for the approved purposes. There are various other instruments such as **federal loans** and the **Coverdell** account or the "**Lifetime Learning Credit**" that parents should discuss with a tax professional as early as possible in order to be fully prepared for the high costs of higher education.

MONEY MATTERS

From an early age, parents should begin discussing with the child basic business and financial matters. In the early years, it can simply be money's uses and the fact that everyone has a job. But as they get older, topics can become more advanced and be about private and public companies, stock ownership, and how climate or politics can affect various financial institutions. To get kids started early in the world of investing, parents can now buy partial shares of stocks at no commissions for kids to own. This will enable a child to buy shares of Apple, for example, and watch the value rise and fall with the vicissitudes of the market. Doing so will begin an early education into investing, a tool that will help them throughout their lives and lead to financial independence.

IN SUMMARY

The cost of education is staggering. America does not have the best track record internationally with our student scores to justify these costs. Parents should strive to get their children into a Montessori school early. As they grow, children should get extra attention in math and writing, with particular emphasis on a "numbers sense" and fractions. Homework should be an important part of the training, and parents should ensure a good place and time has been set aside daily for it. In addition, parents should begin early to teach kids various memory enhancing skills, which will come in handy as the child gets into higher grades. And finally, in that the cost of education is so high, parents should prepare for it early, and begin to teach a financial education to the child.

CHAPTER 15:
DISCIPLINE AND PARENTING STYLES

Even before the child is born, parents undertake the process of shaping and molding the child's behavior with things such as name selection and nursery colors. Once the baby is born, the task of molding behavior is intensified. This could be as simple as reducing the frequency of crying to more complex matters such as better sleeping habits. As children typically progress in years, different techniques are employed to further modify behaviors, some more useful - or harmful - than others. In this chapter, various methods are presented to assist parents in shaping the child into a better, more responsible, and more productive member of society.

OUTBURSTS

Younger children especially do not mean any harm, but part of the trouble is that they may not always be in control of their emotions and/or actions. Dr. Harvey Karp has referred to them as little "cavemen" or "cavewomen" whose right brain, the emotional part, often gets hijacked and compels the cave dweller to engage in the bad behavior. The child often simply cannot help but act like a caveman. We have all seen the child in hysterics over seemingly minor issues. There are ways to deal with it.

Ambassador: Parents can help with these outbursts. A proper and balanced response is the best approach to handling negative behavior. Firm, but kind is the key here. The role of the parent is not to be a friend, but what Dr. Karp refers to as an "ambassador." Connect with respect, speak with respect, treats the child like the human that she is. Parents shouldn't deride or negate a child's feelings. By connecting and treating them with respect, much of the work will have already been done. Let's explore how.

Fast Food Rule: When the child (or anyone for that matter) is upset, parents are encouraged first and foremost to connect with the child on an emotional level. Always repeat back to the child their feelings, indicating to them that you understand what they feel. While doing this, mirror a fraction of their emotional tone as well, the mirroring should be more pronounced for younger children (older children will see through the parents' overdoing it). Merely by being acknowledged, the child's mind will open up and be willing to hear what is next. This can be as simple as kneeling down beside the child and saying in a raised and concerned tone, "Wow, what she said must have really upset you!" It's as simple as a description of what is being observed by the parent. It is not so important what is said but the *way* it is said. When the brain is in such an agitated state, it often cannot understand words, but it can see an emotions and pays attention to gestures and tone of voice. A good rule of thumb is to try to mirror about one-third of the emotion on display. If the child's agitation does not ease up, do not despair. The parent may need to repeat that they understand up to ten times until the message finally gets through to the lost child and she begins her journey back to calmness.

To avoid making things worse, the following responses should be avoided when faced with an outburst:

- Don't ask the child to stop crying when they are upset - they have a right to be upset. Instead, acknowledge the feelings.

- Do not criticize with hurtful words such as "You are being a whiny kid again."

- Do not distract. This merely relays the message that the emotion on display is not important.

- Do not make unfair comparisons, such as "Your brother would never act like this."

- Do not immediately reassure or promise to make it better. Focus on what they are feeling and acknowledge it. They do not need protection from every frustration. Let them be challenged and build resilience by being upset.

- Do not threaten ("Stop or we will leave!").

- Do not question the emotion ("Why are you afraid of spiders?").

- Do not shame the child ("You are a very bad kid for yelling at Aunt Zahra.")

- Do not ignore; children should be acknowledged.

It is only after making the emotional connections that parents should then offer solutions, distraction, consequences, and explanations. It is very important that the child's emotions are not suppressed, and that they are fully acknowledged and permitted. Later, as the child gains a modicum of control over the maelstrom of emotions, parents can explain that every single emotion is proper. Tell the child that emotions are a fact; and that it is the *response* to the emotion that may not be appropriate.

Once parents have connected, the following next steps are recommended:

- **Offer options** ("You may want that toy, but let's look at these two books - which one would you prefer?")

- **Give in to fantasy** ("You wish you could have all of these toys. That would be amazing. Which ones would you play with first?")

- **Share your own feelings** ("When my little daughter throws food on the floor, it really makes me sad that I have to pick it up.")

- **Offer a distraction** ("We can't have that toy, but let's go look at the birds outside.")

- **Reverse praise** - criticize the behavior not the child ("Sometimes even wonderful children do something bad.")

- **Use positivity** (Rather than "No standing on chairs." Use "We like to stand on the floor here.")

- **If a job needs to be done, sandwich it** ("First we will play, then you will pick up your laundry, and then we can do a puzzle.")

OTHER BEHAVIOR MODIFICATION TECHNIQUES

Punishment. Certainly the discipline method having received the most mileage throughout the years is plain and simple punishment. In essence, some negative consequence is imposed on the child for engaging in behaviors that the parent has deemed bad. While punishment may act as deterrent on some level, it may not be the most efficient method of shaping behavior, in that the child may simply learn to avoid engaging in a particular behavior only when the punisher is present.

Corporal Punishment. Corporal punishment is when the child is hit or spanked. There is substantial evidence to suggest that corporal punishment does not work and merely increases the chances that particular behavior will be avoided only in the presence of the punisher. What's more, there is a strong correlation between a child getting hit at home, even if done infrequently, and the likelihood that the child will hit one of her or his peers at school. Besides leading the child to hit their peers, there is some research linking corporal punishment with a number of other general negative behaviors, but the causal link is still being investigated, so we shall reserve that discussion for a later time.

BEST APPROACHES

The most effective method to initiate a change in behavior in the child is a combination of **positive reinforcement** techniques and a **simplified explanation** to help them understand why they need to make a change. Let's explore some methods of doing this.

- **Time-in**. A time-out is where the child is taken away from a certain activity and removed from the attention of those whom she needs most (i.e. the parents). The opposite would then be a time-in. When seeing positive behavior, parents should stop whatever they are doing and focus entirely on the child. Play for ten minutes. Do nothing else. Let the child be rewarded for doing something good.

- **Explain Why**. Once the parent has instructed the child to change a particular behavior, it can be very helpful to explain the rationale behind the requested change. As thinking rational creatures, humans have a greater likelihood of changing certain behaviors once the reason behind the change is understood. Parents are encouraged to explain, even though the explanation may be a bit complex to the child at times. The explanation allows the child to internalize the change and take a level of ownership over it. For example, parents may say, "When you don't pick up your toys, you leave it for me to do, and it is not fair to me because then I won't have time to do my own tasks, and that will make me sad." The next time the child is faced with the option to pick up her toys, the decision will not be whether to pick it up or not, but whether to impose a greater burden on the parents.

- **Rewards**. Another effective approach, related to positive reinforcement, is to grant small rewards for positive behavior. This is not the same thing as bribing a child, which is done preemptively (if you do this, I will give you that), but something to offer once the child behaves in a particular manner. The reward could be something as simple as a small toy or a sticker. Or even marking with a small "X" on the back of the child's hand whenever good behavior is observed. Parents should identify early in the week three behaviors that they would like to see changed. For example, this week may be about saying hello in the morning, picking up toys, and not making a fuss while brushing their teeth. Whenever the positive behavior is observed in relation to these three things, an "X" is placed on the back of the child's hand. When all three positive behaviors are observed in any one day, the child earns a reward, perhaps that sticker. Parents should keep many stickers on hand and let the child choose which sticker. If the "X" system is used, the positive behavior can be reinforced at bedtime by gently reviewing events that led to the X and once again complimenting the child on a job well done.

- **Clear and Consistent Rules**. The human child is wired to push the limits of every single boundary, and will very adeptly cease upon any perceived opportunity or weaknesses to do so. It is therefore imperative that when setting rules, parents follow some basic guidelines. The following is a suggestions:

  1. **Reasonable**: The rules should be reasonable, keeping in mind that especially in the early years the child has very limited impulse control.

  2. **Simple**: The rules should be simple and not so complex so as to not lead to confusion.

  3. **Consistent Enforcement**: Parents should be consistent in the enforcement of the rules. If at any time an exception needs to be made, the exception should be clearly explained. For example, if the "no screens in car" rule needs to be modified because of a long trip, then this should be clearly explained to the child. The explanation could sound something like this: "You know that your normal limit is one hour, but our trip is proving to be very long, so we will give you extra time."

4. **Mixed Messages**: Parents should avoid giving mixed messages, both as a team and as an individual. For example, avoid smiling when setting or enforcing a limit. Instead, the parent should crouch down, remain a little above the child's eye line to maintain a position of authority, and speak with a deep voice and serious face. Another mixed message is when parents do not have a united front. Avoid situations in which one-parent grants permission and the other denies. Children will eventually learn that this is a weakness to exploit and inevitably take advantage of it.

- **Win-Win Compromise**. Parents should strive to create situations that are a "win-win" where both the child and the parent are perceived as winners. The child has an innate sense of fairness, and creating the win-win will reinforce this sense of fairness, allow for a sense of accomplishment, all the while teaching a lesson in compromise. One way to do this is by offering choices, such as two shirts, especially when parents know that the child will definitely refuse one. Another way to do this is by allowing for a negotiation when the parent already knows the outcome. Perhaps begin with a terrible offer, such as telling the child that his or her job is to clean the entire home. When that is immediately rejected, reluctantly give in and say, "Fine you clean your toys and I'll do the rest." This gives the child the win of feeling like a tough negotiator while the parent gets the win of a tidy room.

- **Praise**. A technique that has been proven to have tremendous results in getting the child to modify behavior through praise. Praising positive behavior is very important, but human nature can make this difficult. Parents are more likely to notice and focus on negative behavior rather than the positive. Parents should be cognizant of this. Conversely, parents should be mindful of the fact that excessive praise may come off as unctuous and ultimately prove ineffective. The best approach is whenever positive behavior is observed, praise it right away. Stop whatever you are doing and make a big deal of the positive behavior. "Wow, that was amazing to see you play so well with your sister. I feel so proud to see this." Praise the *behavior* and not the child. Avoid phrases such as "You are such a good boy," since even good boys can sometimes do bad things. If the child makes multiple attempts to modify behavior but does not succeed, this should also be praised. It will only encourage further effort. Parents should avoid the common error with praise whereby the praise is withdrawn or vitiated. Don't take it back. Once praise is given, allow the child to bask in it. Avoid phrases such as, "You did an excellent job . . .but I should not have to remind you."

- **Gossip**. Gossip has a negative connotation, but it is a powerful tool in helping shape the child's behavior. Gossip will serve as indirect praise and can exponentially increase the efficacy of praise. Essentially, the parent praises the child's behavior to a third party, but done in such a manner to allow the child to hear the praise. The third party can be an actual person, or if the child is younger, it can be a feigned phone conversation or even a discussion with a pet or stuffed animal. To add effect, whisper the praise to pretend the child is not intended to hear it. Then, turn back to the child as if nothing had happened and give some direct praise again. Later in the day, to bolster the result, that praise should be repeated to someone else . . . or to a toy or a pet.

- **Star Charts**. In order to recruit the child's help in forging behavior, a star chart can be a very effective tool. To begin, identify three behaviors to work on: one that needs improvement, and two that the child is already able to do well. Explain to the child that you have observed great behavior, but would like to help in getting even better. Then, and with the child's help, create a two-week calendar on a large piece of paper. Let the child choose the color of paper, some stickers, and any other decorations he or she would like. This gives a sense of ownership to the child. Explain to the child that every time that he or she does something good, a sticker will go on the chart. Let the child put the sticker up. Come up with a reward for every ten stickers. As with the

Xs, perhaps a small toy or a funny sticker. Then, show pride in the chart. Perhaps gossip about the behavior to someone (or pet or stuffed animal). Display it clearly so that guests can see it. Be proud of it. Every two weeks, as the child's behavior is changed, come up with a new behavior to forge and repeat.

• **Catch Others Being Good**. A form of praise that parents can employ is praise on other people. Whenever positive behavior is observed in person or in a book or movie or TV show, parents should immediately draw attention to it. Praise that behavior, but avoid making the praise too obvious. Perhaps something as simple as, "Oh look at that girl holding the door open for her father." This will take the attention away from the child's own behavior, but will nevertheless work behind the scenes to effectuate the change parents want.

IN SUM

Parents are encouraged to be patient with children. Most kids are like little cavemen, but they are still human and rational creatures. Parents should follow the suggestions in this chapter on modifying a child's behavior, but by no means to regard this list as exhaustive. Reading Harvey Karp's books, for example, will provide a great training resource. There is certainly no dearth of information out there. With that said, however, parents should be mindful to seek solutions that stem from science and research-based evidence rather than anecdotal or simply because things were "always done this way."

CHAPTER 16:
PROMOTING POSITIVE BEHAVIOR

While a majority of this field manual is dedicated to improving the child's skills as they relate to cognitive and school performance, parents should not overlook the behavior development of a child's internal attitudes as they relate to self esteem, empathy, and so on. While having the skills to do well in school is certainly a necessity in our modern world, research has shown that without the positive attitudes and drive to succeed, the path to success is difficult and rife with seemingly insurmountable obstacles.

Children in general are resilient and are able to bounce back from defeats and failures fairly quickly. This is a handy trait, as they are faced on a daily basis with tasks they have hardly begun to grasp, let alone mastered, and failure or defeat is a common occurrence for them. This resilience and optimism tends to wane as the child grows, which can affect the child's success both in and out of the classroom. Learning to maintain a positive and optimistic attitude has been shown to be a significant factor in the child's success, and it is parents and teachers who have the biggest impact on helping the child develop and maintain this attitude.

The general pattern of learning goes something like this: the child learns new information, and then applies that new information to different problems. Inevitably, the child encounters various failures in the application of this new knowledge, which leads her to find the gaps in knowledge, fills in those gaps, and attempt to solve the problems again. Trouble occurs in the phase after failing in discovering the gaps of knowledge, and it is here that the child may despair and give up, often attributing the failure to some internal shortcoming and does not take that next step, which is to set out to fill in the gaps in knowledge. The child may think they are just not "good enough" or smart enough and begin to show a lack of interest in future studies.

TRY HARDER

Various studies have shown the effects of focusing the child's attention to how hard the child tried rather than some innate internal ability when measuring success or failure. It was shown in one study, for example, that when children repeated the phrase, "I got that right - that means I tried hard," and "I got that wrong, that means I need to try harder," showed large improvements in reading skills over a very short time period. Parents are therefore encouraged to teach this to the child. Have the child repeat this mantra, so that it becomes a part of success or failure even when not in the presence of the parents. Parents should bolster this mindset throughout the day. When observing the child doing something well, parents should repeat, "That was great, it means you tried hard," and similarly, "No, that wasn't correct, it means you must try harder." This will shift the focus from something internal (i.e. not within the child's control) to something that the child can control (the amount and quality of hard work associated with learning the task).

BOOST SELF ESTEEM

A strong level of self-esteem has been proven to have big benefits for children, both in and out of the classroom. Parents can be involved from an early age in guiding and boosting a child's self-esteem so that when the challenges of school and life inevitably push back, the child will be better prepared to overcome them. Below are some examples of how to do this:

Playing the "Boob." As Dr. Karp puts it, at an early age the parent is encouraged to "play the boob" to the child (as described by way of example below). It helps the child feel smart and confident compared to her "klutzy" parents. There are a number of ways that parents can go about doing this:

- **Strong high fives**. Obviously more suited for younger children, but the parent will exaggerate the pain associated with the high five from the child. The parent can even blow on the hand to pretend to lessen the pain.

- **Be blind**. Parents will look for things that are obviously right in front of them. And when the child finds it, praise them loudly.

- **Be a klutz**. Drop something that the child hands to you over and over.

- **Be confused**. When putting on shoes, for example, be confused about where the other shoe goes. On hands? On ears?

- **Be forgetful**. Pretend you have forgotten what they just requested. Did you say you want eggs? Oh right cereal. Wait, what was it that you wanted again?

- **Be incorrect**. Rather than saying let's eat an apple say "Let's eat this motorcycle." And let the child correct you.

- **Be weak**. Perhaps in a wrestling match, let the child win to show how strong he or she is.

Ask For Help. Whenever possible, parents should ask the child for help. This will signal that the parent believes in the child and that the child can do the task. It could be holding the screwdriver or the whisk to mix the pancake mix.

Give Choice. Whenever possible, present choices to the child and help them make decisions. But don't present too many choices, as it may overwhelm a younger child especially. Also, do not present a choice that parents are willing to disregard.

Something the Child is Good At. Parents should help the child discover some activity or thing in which the child feels confident and capable. For some it may be athletics. For others it may be music or art. Find what it is and help foster the child's skills. This will build confidence and spill over into other parts of the child's life.

Facing Defeats. While there may be a natural tendency to protect children from all defeats, it is important to expose the child to some minor defeats in order to teach necessary resilience. Let the child get frustrated and find a way to work it out. Parents must resist the urge to help in every situation. For example, when the child is working on a puzzle and she just cannot figure out a way to make a particular piece fit, let the child struggle and try to figure it out on her own. If she just isn't getting it in the end, perhaps offer a little help, but ultimately let the child make the final move. On the playground, avoid rushing in to help a child climb a playground structure, and let the child fail a few times and learn from those defeats.

Praise Effort. Whenever possible, parents should praise a child's *effort* in achieving certain accomplishments, rather than the accomplishment itself. That's not to say the accomplishment should be downplayed in any way, but the bulk of the praise should be on the work the child put into the success. Related to this, whenever parents notice hard work and concentration, the child should be praised for it. It can be as simple as, "I can see you are trying really hard with this and am proud of you." When they persist in the face of failure, notice it and praise them for it.

IN SUM

Life is hard, especially for children who are constantly facing the frustrations of learning new skills and the failure of applying those skills to their world. Parents should strive to be the bulwark against all of these negative forces. Teach children that their successes are a result of their hard work and determination, and not some innate ability that they are born with. Encourage self esteem and personal growth by playing the boob, giving them choices, and helping them find their strengths. Let them occasionally fail in order to build resilience. The skills they take away from it will work in concert with the cognitive tools they are given throughout the remainder of this manual.

CHAPTER 17:
ENLIGHTENMENT

There was a time when the daily struggle of humanity was against the brutal and harsh natural environment, strife with saber tooth tigers and ice ages, and the goal of all parenting endeavors was to rear offspring capable of physically surviving long enough to reproduce. And while humanity has gained a certain level of dominance over this cruel harsh world, that primeval goal is still as important as ever. But with the evolving needs of humanity, it is no longer just about physical survival. It now becomes equally important to raise children that understand their role in society, both as law abiding members of things as they are as well as harbingers of change. It is thus up to parents to guide and teach children about the various shortcomings of humanity and to empower and enable children with the right tools to tackle these shortcomings. This chapter lists a few of the topics that parents should consider discussing with the child.

MALE AND FEMALE

From an evolutionary historic perspective, the roles of the male human were clearly different than that of the female in the day-to-day affairs. The physical size and strength disparity between males and females allowed the males to quickly fall into dominant roles and gain power over the female. This of course was exasperated by the protracted periods of pregnancy in which the female found herself, which in essence rendered the female members of the species useless in terms of hunting and warding off predators. Over time, this dominant submissive duality becomes ensconced in the structure of human civilizations. The world required brute force to conquer and that's what the male offered, and this dialectic served us well. But that was thousands of years ago and times have changed. Technology has, by and large, rendered brute force useless. The female member of the species, even while pregnant and on the verge of childbirth, can be as effective in society as any male. Women are now in every single profession and have proven just as capable as any man.

Unfortunately, the anachronistic dance of dominant/submissive male/female roles has persisted despite our technological advancements. As statistics can reveal with the most rudimentary of searches, a woman encounters much more difficulty in achieving the same goals a man does. Women in the work force are much more likely to experience less pay, greater harassment, and bigger obstacles than their male counterparts. Much of this is based on the systems that are in place in human society; but much of this is also learned by children from observing parents, friends, teachers, and the media. Boys are often encouraged to grow big and be stronger and succeed, while girls are pushed to be attractive (presumably for the boys), become domesticated and learn to support the male. This does not just limit females, but also males and the species as a whole. It therefore becomes crucial for parents to address these toxic ideas and nip them in the bud.

- **Books and Female Protagonists**. A recent examination of typical bookstore shelves demonstrated that there is a dearth of children's books in which females are listed as protagonists and who do not require a male's help to accomplish their goals. A majority of published books portray girls in roles of princesses or some other role in which any position of power is merely a product of the help of a man (a princess, after all, is only what she is because of her father the king). The problem with princesses is twofold: 1.) the books about princesses almost always show the princess in a submissive and dire position and a male (often a prince) is needed to save her, and 2.) the princess gets her very importance not by any personal endeavors or accomplishments, but by the circumstance of her fortuitous birth. She doesn't *do* anything; she is just born into wealth and privilege. This shifts the focus away from what a girl can do or change in her life to what the girl is given by the mere happenstance of her birth. Parents are encouraged to seek out books that show girls in a positive and empowered light. Increase the demand and authors will meet the need. Look for books that are about girls. Whether the child is a boy or a girl, they should be exposed to a 50/50 split of books where some have male leads and some female. There are some books that are just too good to pass up, and in such circumstances, while parents read to the child, and especially before the child knows how to read, there is nothing wrong with furtively changing pronouns to make the lead character female. In *Goodnight Moon*, for example, there is no reason that either the small rabbit or the little mouse must be male.

- **Pink.** Typically when parents discover that the child is male, the room decorations inevitably become blue, and if female, pink. Looking back in history over just a brief period, however these colors were actually reversed, and pink was considered the dominant masculine color and blue the effete weaker one. Today, as girls grow up, they almost always describe pink as their favorite color. A little girl's entire play area, from the sheets on the bed to the paint on the wall, is saturated with pink. A boy, on the other hand, is given the remainder of the colors in the spectrum. This way of thinking is outdated and limiting to girls. Parents should strive to promote all of the colors for both sexes.

- **Toys**. Toys have generally become a great source of the divide between boys and girls. A brief survey of any girls' toy bin will reveal a collection almost entirely dedicated to skills required to be a mother. The majority of toys will be in the form of beauty and makeup products to initially attract a child's father, small babies to practice mothering, and kitchenware to learn early how to cook for the child and child's father. A boy's room, conversely, is full of every single other type of toy. There will be cars, trucks, airplanes, building blocks, puzzles, games, and so on. As previously mentioned, this is the very thing that propagates the division between boys and girls, pushing girls towards the maternal roles and the boy towards every other role, which includes builder, doctor, someone that is outside of the house and dominant and in charge of his own life. What's more, there is ample evidence that certain toys can aid in a child's cognitive development, and by keeping girls from such toys, it merely exasperates the problem. Below is an excellent tool to determine whether a toy is for a boy or a girl:

HOW TO TELL IF A TOY IS FOR BOYS OR GIRLS: A GUIDE

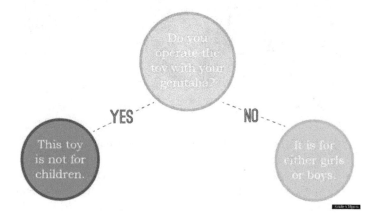

Do you operate the toy with your genitalia?

YES — This toy is not for children.

NO — It is for either girls or boys.

- **Beauty**. Continuing with this theme, as men are pushed to become conquerors of their world, women are pushed to be domestic and to accentuate their beauty in order to catch and then keep a man. Girls are often praised for their looks and their clothes, boys on the other hand are praised for their accomplishments, strength and speed. Girls in books almost invariably are introduced by the level of beauty they possess. Beauty becomes dominant in a girl's world. Parents buy makeup and play lipstick for girls at an early age. In essence, girls begin to learn at an early age that their own face is not good enough and they must purchase certain products in order to hide their natural face. Boys can put their own natural face on display, but girls must cover up. They are not good enough on their own. As girls grow older, they will hyper focus on their physical beauty, feeding into the "Selfie culture" that is not about where they are, but what they *look* like where there are. Parents are therefore encouraged to shift the focus away from physical beauty. Let beauty be only a fraction of the praise she receives. Instead, focus the praise on her effort, her speed, and her strength. Do not prevent her from getting dirty where boys are allowed to run free (mud puddles, for example). Parents should explain this to the rest of the family, for they too play a crucial role and are often the source of much of the beauty compliments. Offer them this simple analogy in which a girl has five or six glass jars, each labeled for one of the traits she has (beauty, perseverance, curiosity, strength, and so on). Every time she receives a compliment about one of those traits, a token is tossed into its respective jar. Over the years, the one that is filled the most will often lead to the trait from which the girl will derive her worth. If you fill the beauty jar, that is how the girl will define herself. If you fill the strength jar, she will see herself as strong.

- Others. Parents should also prepare the child for the outside world when sexism is rampant. Have them look out for it and be prepared for it. Quiz the child regularly and ask which colors are only for girls/boys, and then teach them to reply that "all colors" are for girls/ boys and "all toys" are for girls/boys. Teach them to watch for the sexism they encounter in the media where, for example, it is always the man that drives the car, women are often portrayed as the weaker sex, and women are portrayed only in relation to men (the wife, the sister, the nurse to the doctor, the queen of the king). Research and then explain to children that movies all receive a score on something called the *The Bechdel Test*, which asks whether a particular book or movie or television show features "at least two women who talk to each other about something other than a man." Most programs fail this test.

- **Play**. Parents are encouraged to find playmates for their children of both sexes. The tendency seems to be for boys to play with boys and girls to play with girls. This only further alienates the sexes from one another and leads to misunderstanding as they grow older. Select play dates not just with boys for boys, but mix it up. Let them learn to play with the other sex.

• **Gifts**. Be mindful of the presents and toys that the child receives. Give boys dolls -- they too need to learn how to be good parents. Give girls trucks and airplanes -- they too need to learn to master the world. Remind friends and family of this as well.

RACISM

Much like sexism, racism is rampant in society, and often traces its roots to evolutionary survival skills. Racism primarily stems from the fear of foreigners who historically were a threat to the small hunter/gatherer groups in which humans found themselves in prehistoric times. Those that were not in your group were seen as a threat, competing for scarce resources of food and shelter. But just as the evolutionary forces that led to the difference in men and women are now obsolete for the most part, so too is it true for racism. The human species has connected with one another all over the world. There is no real distinction between an "us" and a "them." As such, humans are a global group, and parents should spread that message to children. Teach them at an early age that we are not different. We only look different. The differences in our culture do not make us different, they only show that our families hail from different parts of the world before the world became one.

MINDFULNESS

Mindfulness cannot be avoided in today's culture. Nearly every program or school now has some level of mindful practice. Research has repeatedly shown the benefits of mindfulness, going as far as suggesting that the very structure of the brain is modified with regular sitting practice. Mindfulness is merely being present and in the moment. While the typical response to stimuli is to wander off with thoughts and think of the past or the future that is associated with something currently happening, mindfulness merely teaches to come back to the present, notice the body and the breath, and examine the physical reactions to the stimuli. Doing this every day can change the child's life. It will allow for better impulse control and emotional regulation. In the book "Sitting Still Like a Frog," Eline Snel gives various methods and techniques on how best to incorporate mindfulness into a daily routine. Parents are encouraged to read this book and employ the short exercises with children.

NATURE DEFICIT DISORDER (NDD)

As society has gotten more technologically advanced, kids are spending less time away from technology. Indeed, Richard Louc in his wonderful book "Nature Deficit Disorder" coined the term "NDD" (a play off of Attention Deficit Disorder, or ADD) to describe the general mindset of children who have been raised without adequate nature interaction. Research has consistently demonstrated the many benefits of regular exposure to nature, yet modern metropolitan society offers so little opportunity for it. Parents thus need to find time on a regular basis to get their child out into nature. This generally means without any toys and structure, and they will find that the child will roam and climb trees and be difficult to convince to finally leave the forests. Parents are encouraged to spend time in nature doing something as basic as a short hike, to longer hikes with picnics packed in a backpack, to something even more elaborate like an actual camping trip. This can be made even more fun by inviting the child's classmates, neighbors, or other friends and family.

IN SUM

The demands of our society are great, and as electronics become more ubiquitous, our lives will continue to change. At times for the better, but there are also dangers. Parents are encouraged to discuss the changing roles of humans, and in particular how we have and should shed our anachronistic ideas about the sexes and outsiders. Children should be taught to become better citizens. As often as possible, families should get outdoors and help children connect with their natural world. As in the famous Dr. Seuss book, *The Lorax*, it won't be long before all of the trees are gone.

CHAPTER 18:
PARENTAL UNIT BOND

It should become clear by now to parents who have read this manual that proper human childcare is a full-time all-consuming endeavor. It seems that at every turn there is a lesson to teach and an activity for which to prepare. The whole process taxes emotional, financial, and temporal resources, rendering parents exhausted, short fused, and often in dire financial straits. Once the kids are put to bed (and provided that they remain in bed) the exhausted parents will hardly have sufficient energy to move, let alone engage with one another in much needed couples' bonding. This can often lead to marriage strain and discord and ultimately divorce in many instances.

Raising a child is hard. It is likely one of the most difficult endeavors humans have ever undertaken. But it is crucial that the parental unit take adequate measure to care not just for the child, but also for itself as a team and also as individual members of the team. A well-rested parental unit can be much more effective, especially when the individual members of the team are happy with themselves as individuals and with one another as a couple. Parents would be best served to remember that at some point, the child will leave the family to venture out into the world, and what will remain is either a happy vibrant couple or the ghost shell of what once was.

Additionally, parents should keep another important factor in mind. As children mature into adulthood, they will take the lessons, both explicit and implicit, that they learned at home into the world with them. They will hopefully remember all of lessons about fractions and memory enhancement and nutrition, but there is also another big lesson they will take with them into the great expanse: how to be a spouse and a parent. Indeed, much of how they behave or expect as a parent or a spouse will be based on the silent lessons they learned while living at home in those formative years.

With this in mind, below are some suggestions for parents to employ:

- **Calling Spouse "Mommy" or "Daddy"**. As instructions and directions are repeated throughout the day, everything is about the child. When parents say, "Go give this to Daddy," or "Did you ask Mommy already?" they are referring to one another as they relate to the child (Mommy is to child, and daddy is to child). Doing this all day, it becomes tempting and requires less energy to simply refer to the other parent by that same moniker of "mommy" or "daddy." But parents should take great care to avoid referring to one another by those names. This, in essence, creates a world where their sole purpose of existence is to parent, completing pushing their roles as spouses and individuals to the side. While it certainly may seem that this is practically what happens anyway, couples should remember that the household will thrive best if the parents retain their identity as a couple and as individuals. Couples are thus advised to refer to one another with whatever pet names were used prior to the birth of the child. If it was "Fancy Face," then "Fancy Face" it should continue.

- **Alone Time**.   Over the course of human civilization, population clusters have grown more and more dense, creating a world where daily human contact is nearly inevitable. This is of course accentuated in a home with children, and parents are rarely granted an opportunity to be alone. But this alone time is crucial to the spirit of the human. Indeed, there are numerous philosophical books dedicated to the practice of solitude. Major American historical figures such as Walt Whitman and Henry David Thoreau are celebrated for taking time away from society to relish in their solitude. According to Psychology Today, solitude can provide:

  - An opportunity for the brain to reboot, giving it a break from the always "on" state that it finds itself as a parent.

  - A boost in concentration and productivity by taking away all of the latest and loudest distractions.

  - An opportunity to find one's own voice away from the group-think mentality.

  - Time for deep thinking about life and philosophical ideas in general.

  - Helps in the working out of problems more effectively by allowing time to think of solutions.

  - Better quality relationships with a significant other by allowing the individual to think through problems in the relationship and come up with creative solutions.

- Spending time alone is a very important part of what makes humans most effective. Parents should find time on a daily basis just for themselves. This can be in the form of a gym workout, taking a walk, or even the commute to work or the restroom (provided the child does not come knocking). With this in mind, each parent should also be mindful of the other partner's need for solitude and help provide opportunities for them. The dance of parenthood is best and easiest when both members are at their best.

- **Screen Time - Couples**. That smartphones and tablets are highly addictive is axiomatic by now. People spend most of their waking hours staring at screens. And just as it can harm the child, its pernicious effects are felt by parents as well. As most can attest, after a grueling and exhausting day and the children have been put finally to bed, parents will plop down in front of the television and get lost in their favorite shows. While this zoning out and relaxing can certainly have its benefits, it also serves the role of not allowing for important personal interaction between the couple. Therefore, the guideline is that once or twice a week, parents should have a technology free night and focus on one another. This time can be spent just talking, but can also be spent on exercise, board games, or even taking it as a rare opportunity to be intimate with one another.

- **Screen Time - Alone**. Indeed, receding screen time is something that the individual members of the couple should focus on even when alone. Try to avoid constantly being on the phone, even when in line at the bank, grocery store, at home, or in the car. Although no one likes being bored, yet research has actually revealed that boredom provides cognitive benefits on the brain. Most of human creativity has been bred out of boredom. Put away the smartphones. "Veg out" as often as possible. The benefits of the occasional period of ennui can outweigh the benefits of whatever new information there is on social media.

- **Exercise**. Getting regular exercise is crucial for the child. That advice is equally applicable to parents. An unhealthy parent is a useless parent. As airlines advise passengers to put on their own oxygen mask before helping others, so too should parents take care of themselves so that they can effectively help their children. This means spending consistent regular time exercising. It can be something as formal and structured as the gym, but it can also be simpler such as taking the stairs rather than an elevator or escalator, parking at a spot farther away, and so on. Keeping parents' bodies healthy will ultimately help the child.

- **Rule Of 2-2-2**. Finding time for one another for parents is not an easy task, but the Rule of 2-2-2 may help organize that time. In essence, it breaks down as follows:

  - Every two weeks, parents should find alone time for themselves. This can mean hiring a sitter or recruiting a family member so that they can go on a "date night." Once on the date, avoid talking about children. Focus on one another and reconnect. Find out about each other's fears, passions, and ambitions. People evolve, desires and goals change, so this provides an excellent opportunity to stay in pace with one another's changes.

  - Every two months plan a getaway for a weekend. It does not need to be an extravagant trip; renting a hotel room on the other side of town can work just fine. Walk around your own city or town like a tourist. Spend the weekend together, eat at a restaurant, and drink during the day.

  - Every two years go away for a week. This of course also has budgetary limitations, but find an opportunity to spend alone time for a few days away from the children and the hustle and bustle of daily work and home routines. It will provide an excellent opportunity to rest, reconnect, and reboot.

- **Affection on Display.** What parents do and say to one another will have a big effect on how children act in their own relationships someday. Parents should be mindful to avoid speaking harshly to one another, especially when the child is around. Take great care to avoid hurtful and harsh words. Conversely, parents are encouraged not to hide affection towards one another. Put it on wide display. Let the children see that a respectful and caring relationship can exist between a couple, even in the miasma and vortex of a house full of children. Hold hands in public and speak softly to one another. They will notice.

IN SUM

Raising children is a very difficult task. It truly does require a village's help. It also requires the individual members of this village to be healthy and capable of the task. Parents mustn't lose sight of their own wellbeing in the process. Not only should they make an effort to stay healthy as individuals, they should also work on being a strong and loving couple. Spend time alone and with one another. Take breaks from the kids—the kids will thank you for it.

CHAPTER 19:
THINGS TO CARRY

DIAPER BAG

The best ones have a waterproof lining and lots of pockets. Parents are also encouraged to place leakable items (cream, etc.) inside plastic bags to prevent a mess. Below is a list of standard items to keep in a diaper bag, but parents should feel free to modify to fit their own needs:

- A changing pad on which to lay the child. Even where public restrooms have a changing table that does not mean it has been kept clean.

- Wet wipes can serve not only to clean the baby's bottom, but also for cleaning the face, hands, and whatever else.

- Soap or hand sanitizer.

- Extra diapers.

- Small plastic bags in which to dispose of diapers as necessary.

- Snacks, the specific nature depending on age of child.

- Milk, water.

- Clean pacifiers

- Extra clothing.

- Sun hat.

- Diaper rash cream.

- Sunscreen.

- First aid kit.

- Children's Tylenol, because you never know.

- Books, toys.

OVERNIGHT BAG

Going somewhere overnight would require the same contents as the diaper bag, with a few additional items. Parents should pack the bag a few days early, but at any rate, have this list handy to mark off:

- Baby monitor

- Overnight crib

- Additional clothing and diapers

- Charging chords

LONG ROAD TRIPS AND VACATIONS

The contents would be the same as the overnight bag, but add things to entertain the children on the trip itself:

- Snacks just for the road

- A surprise bag - can be a simple paper bag filled with a few new cheap $1 toys and snacks

- Games

- Tablets for movies

- Books

- Puzzle and coloring books

- Printed out sheets for various road games such as Bingo in which someone marks off a box every time a road item (such as a tractor, school bus, barn, and so on) is seen.

CAMPING

Besides regular camping supplies and the lists above, the HCP team should consider the following items:

- Outdoor toys

- Bikes and helmets

- Frisbee

- Water toys

- Small backpack for toys, games, puzzles

IN CAR

A lot of time will be spent in the car. A good rule of thumb is not to allow the child to have screen time in a car unless it is for a trip that is longer than two hours. Therefore, there should be sufficient items to keep the child occupied:

- Plenty of books and magazines (High Five, Chirp, or National Geographic Kids, as examples)

- Puzzles and brain twister books

- A basket full of toys

- Water

- Wipes and sanitizers

- Paper towels

- Tissues

- Gum for the mountain drives

- Plastic bag for motion sickness

- First aid kid
- Balls

CHAPTER 20:
GENERAL TIMELINE

While there are no hard and fast rules on when the child is to take up certain activities, and the individual needs and resources available to parents will dictate much of it, below is a general guideline of when to introduce various activities:

Age 1

- Swim Lessons

- Plenty of songs and signing and music

- Picture books, stories

Age 2 - 4

- Books slightly more advanced

- Dance lessons

- Tricycles

Age 4-5

- Music lessons (piano, etc.)

- Teach how to ride bike without training wheels

5 +

- Start teaching about money and finances

- Begin teaching about the human body and its needs

- Martial Arts

Conclusion

A lot of information and ground has been covered in this manual. There is much to do for parents as well as children. Schedules need to be made, routines established, practices to attend. But there is one important thing that should be remembered throughout the period that parents are privileged enough to be around the child. The best childhood is an unhurried childhood. While parents may follow the various guidelines presented in this manual, it should be remembered that children benefit from unstructured play. It can be easy to get lost in the soccer practices, piano recitals, and homework hours, but parents should take good care to ensure the child enjoys their childhood. Create opportunities for the child to have fun. In the Italian Oscar-winning movie *Beautiful Life*, a father creates a happy and unhurried childhood for his son, even in the most horrific of circumstances. Endeavor to maximize the potential of a child, but balance it with the joys of a halcyon childhood. It is with this balance that your child will thrive.

To every parent and child in the military and beyond, "Hooah!"